# IRELAND

PHOTOGRAPHS BY ELIZABETH KRAMER

THIS IS PART OF THE **VISITING** SERIES.

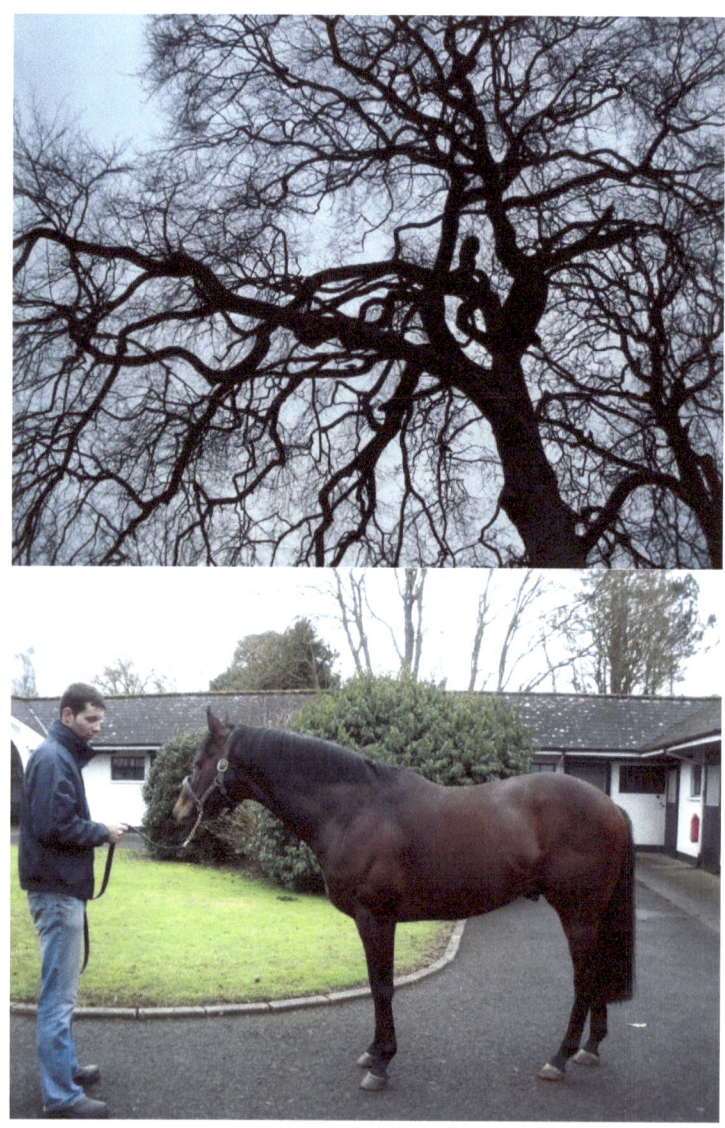

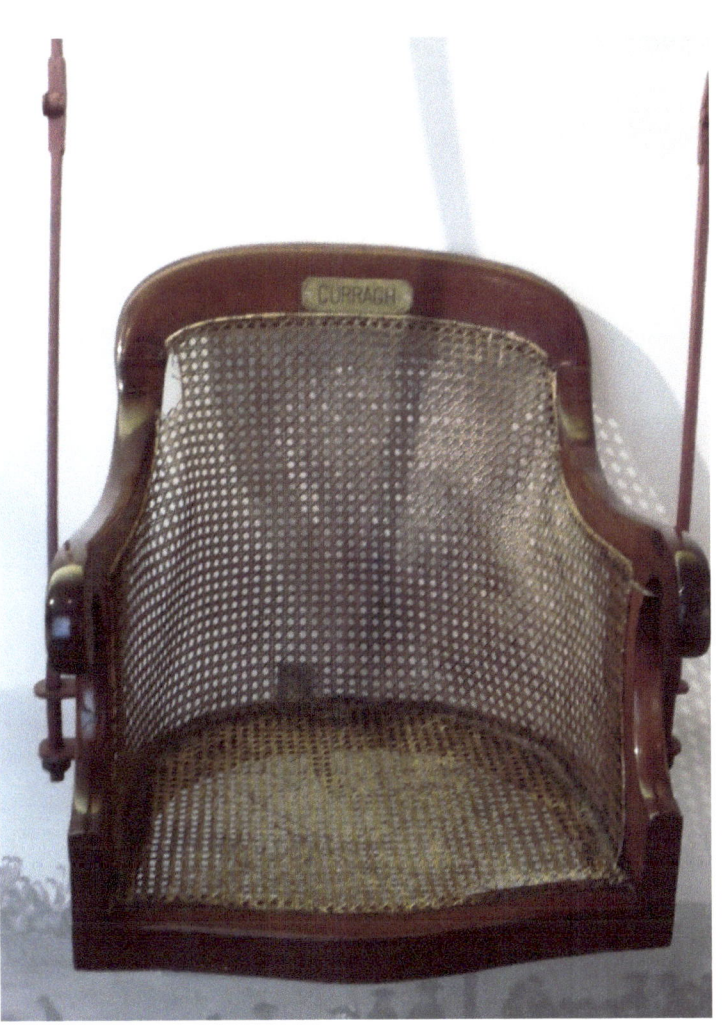

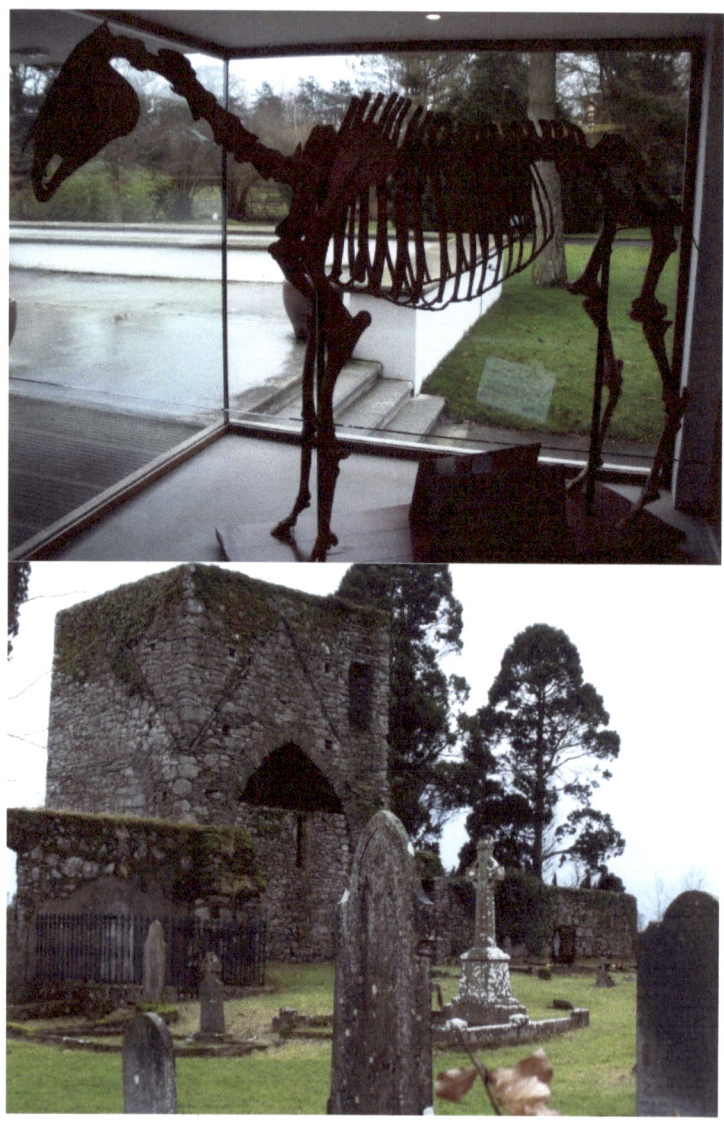

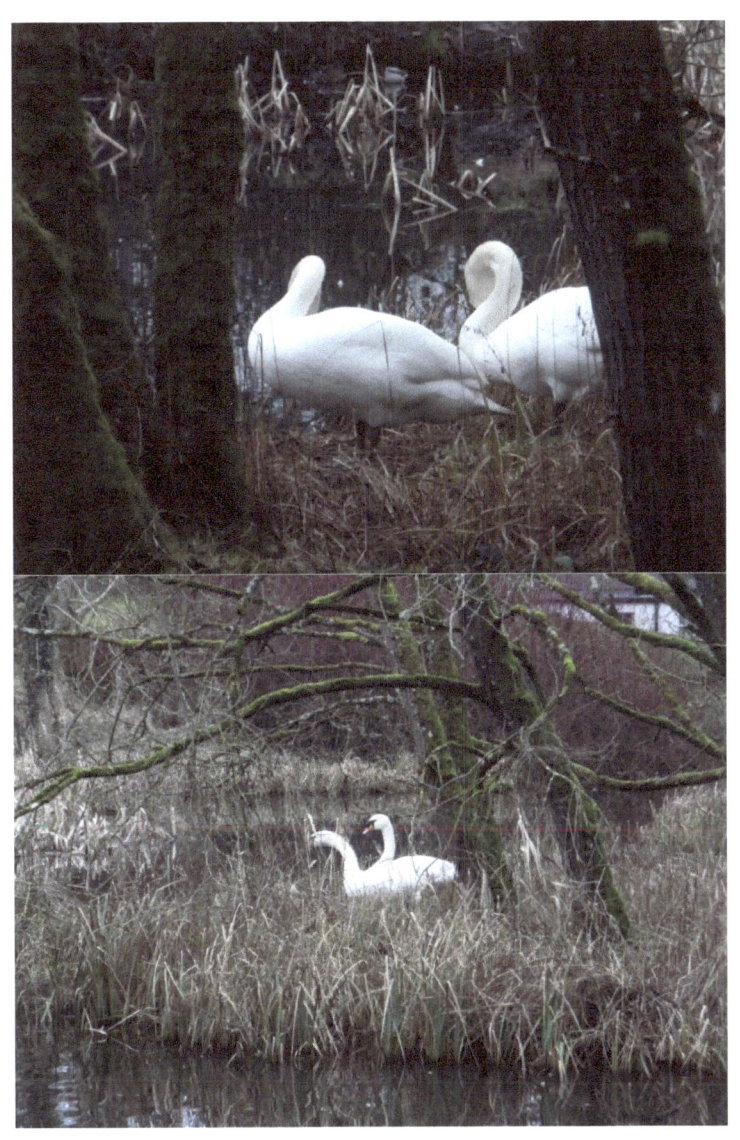

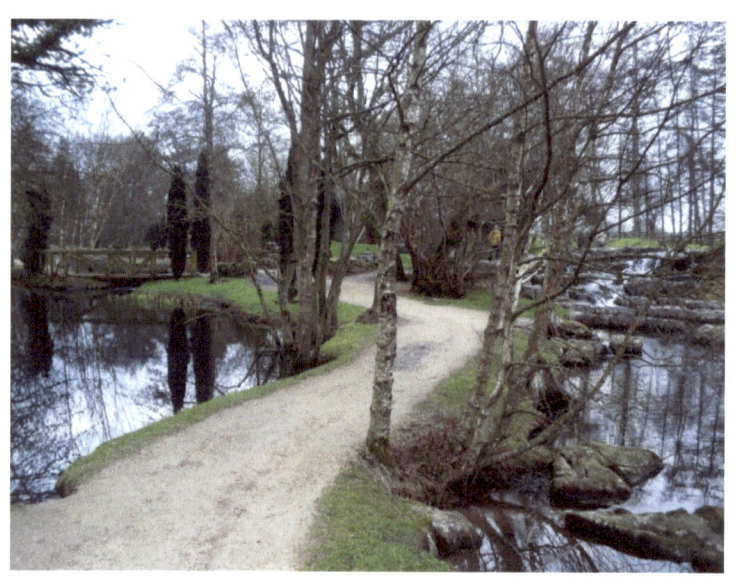

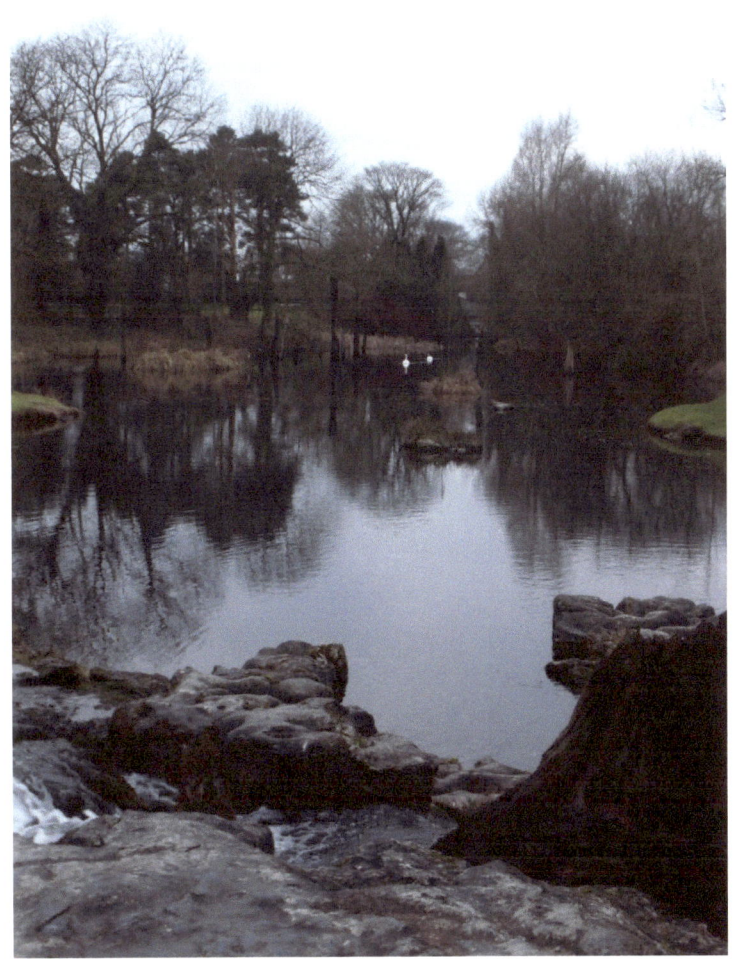

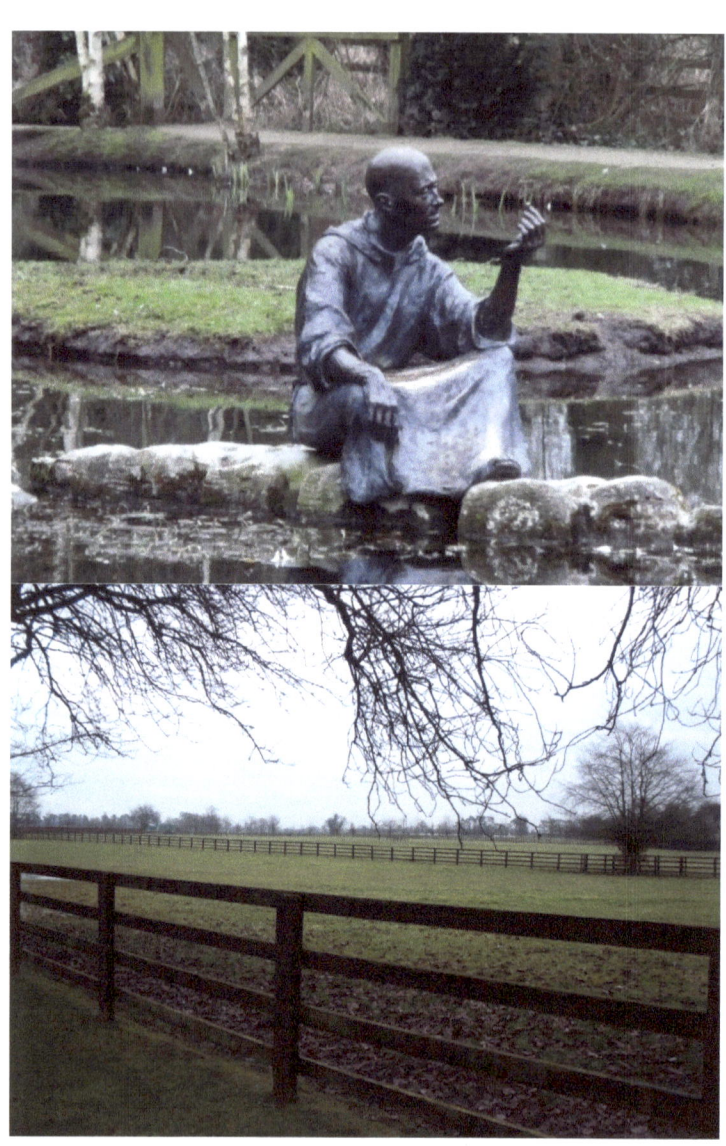

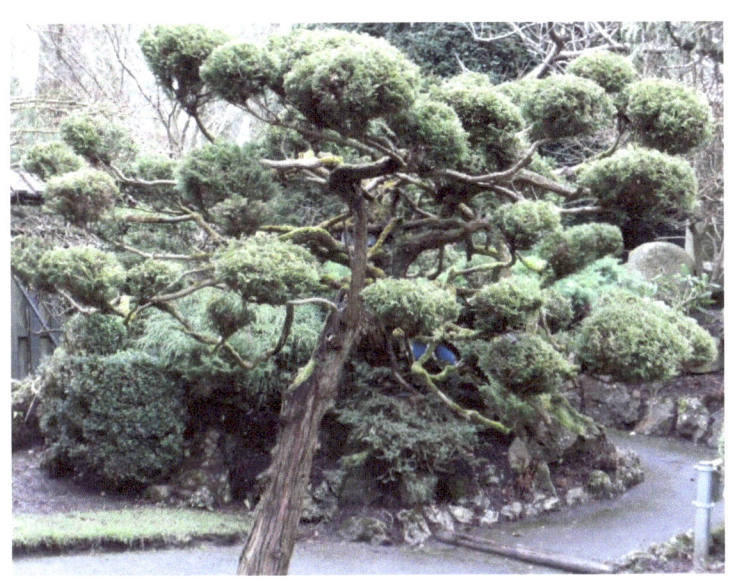

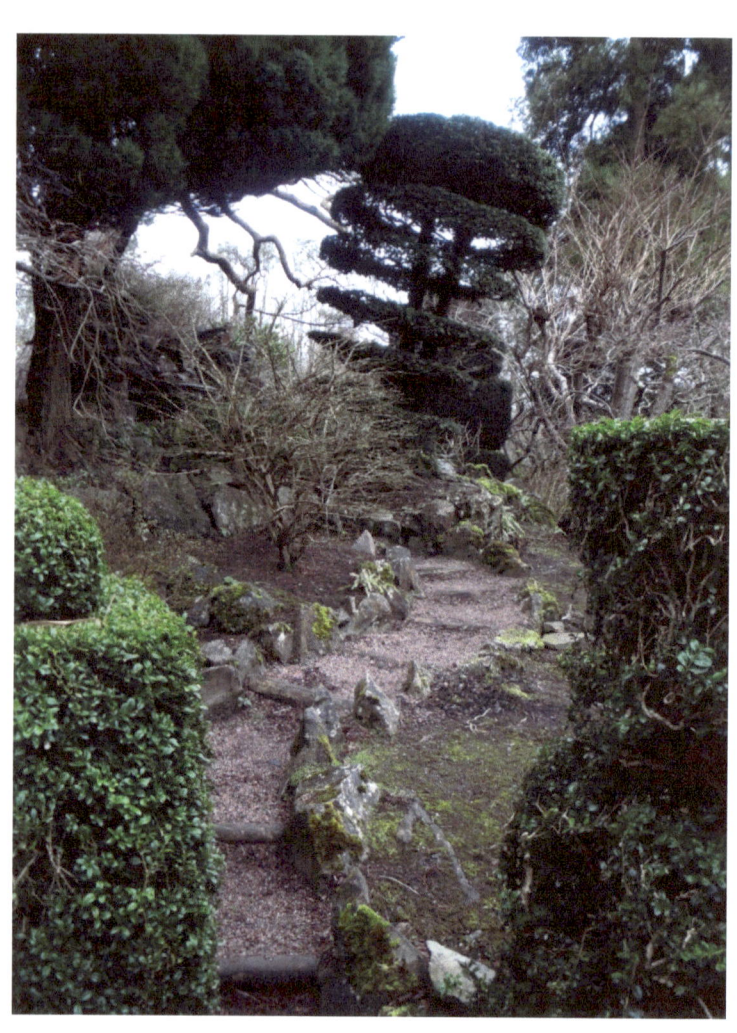

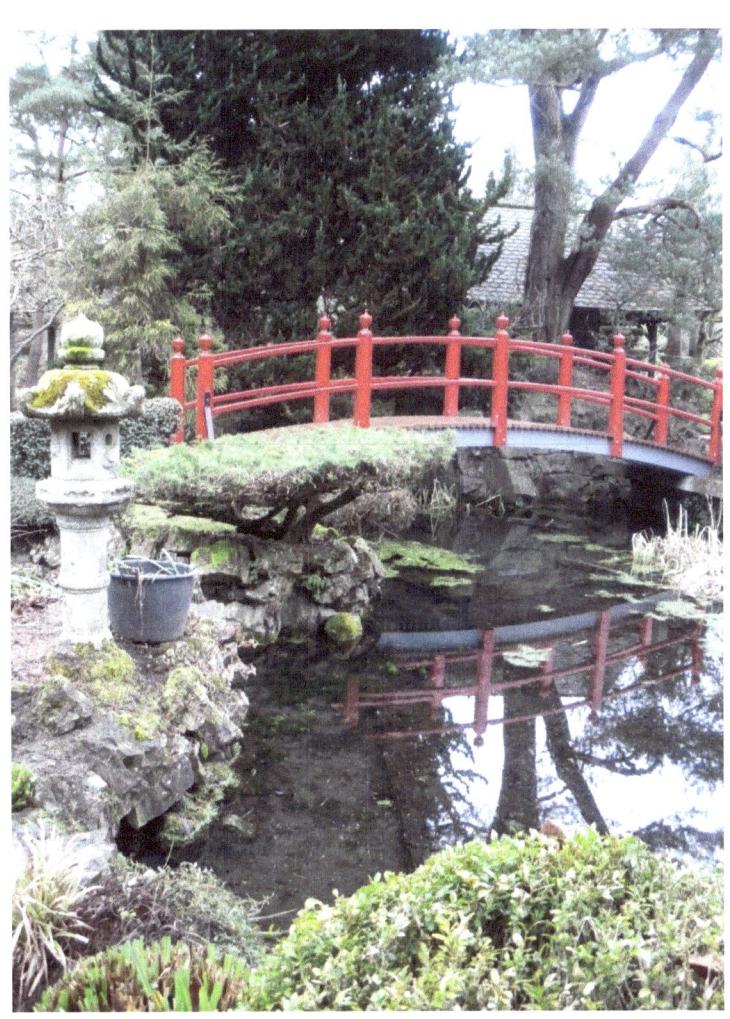

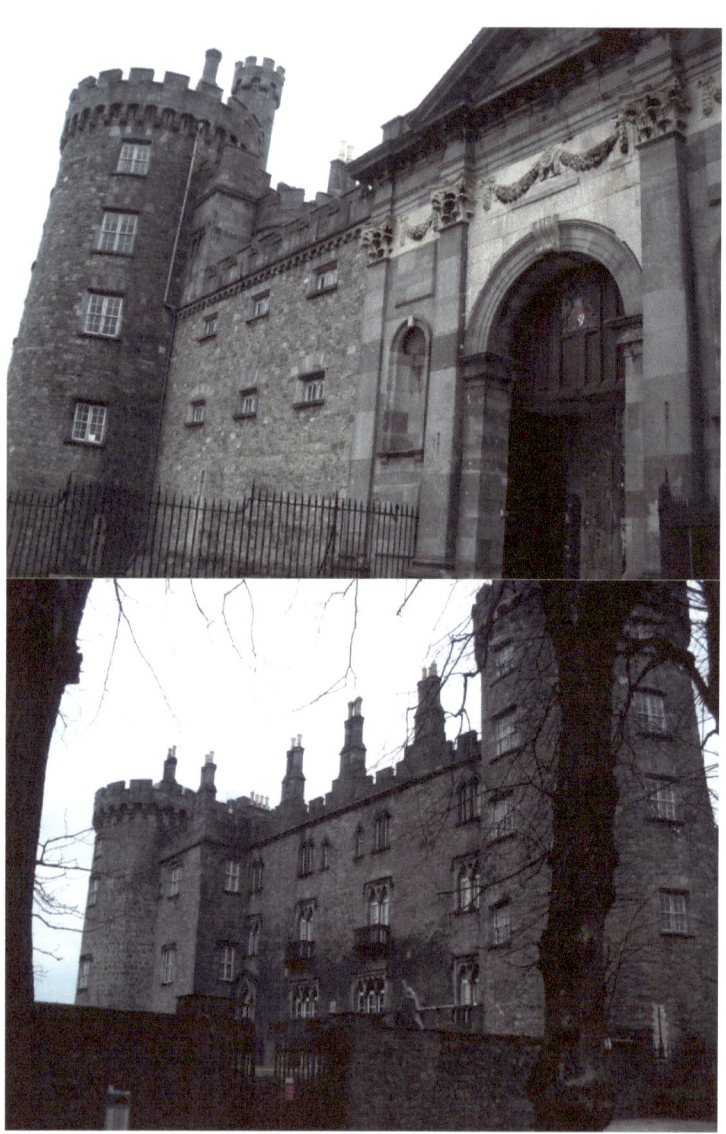

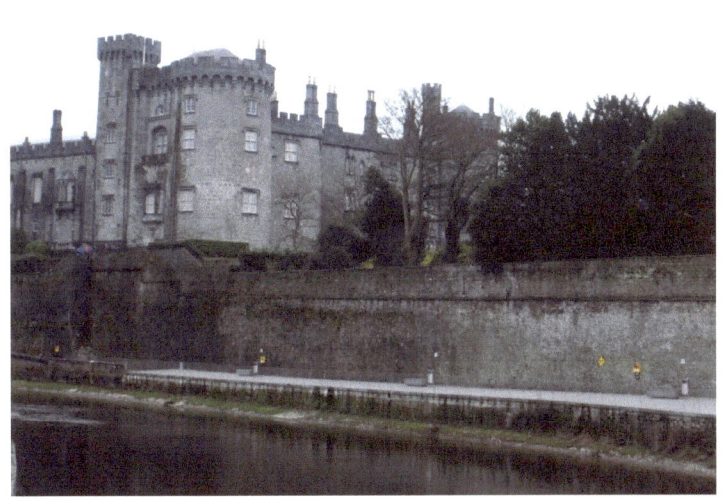

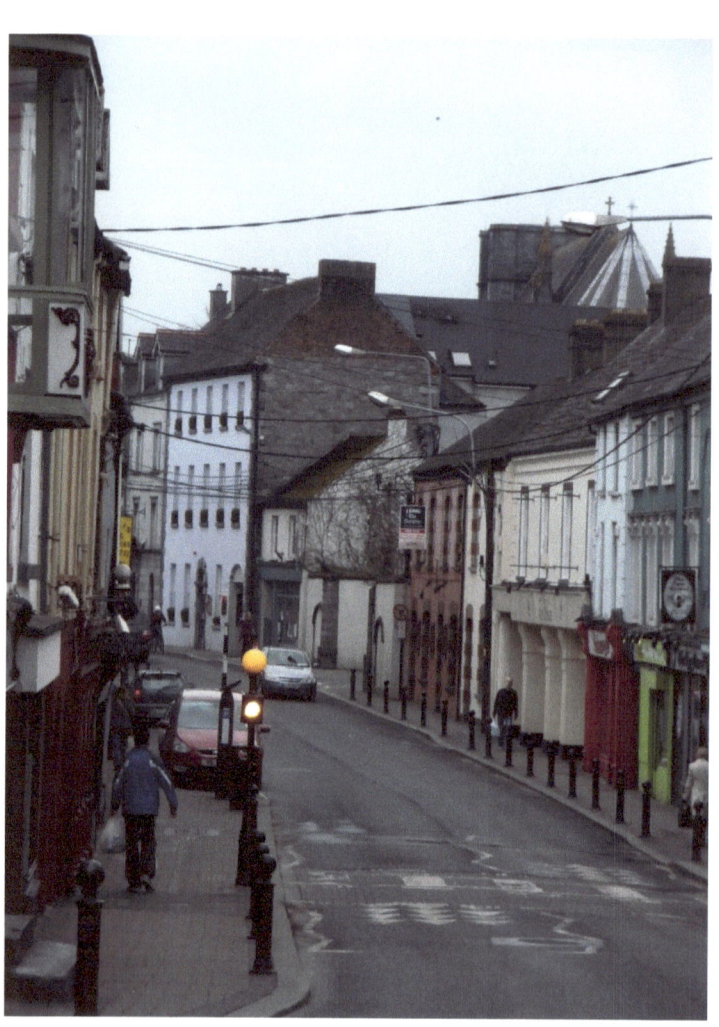

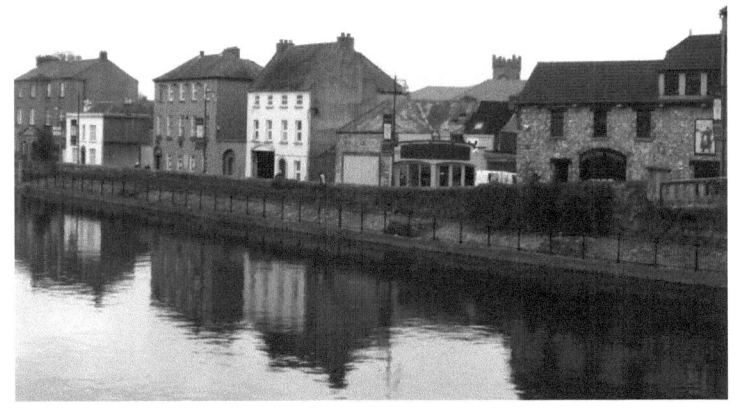

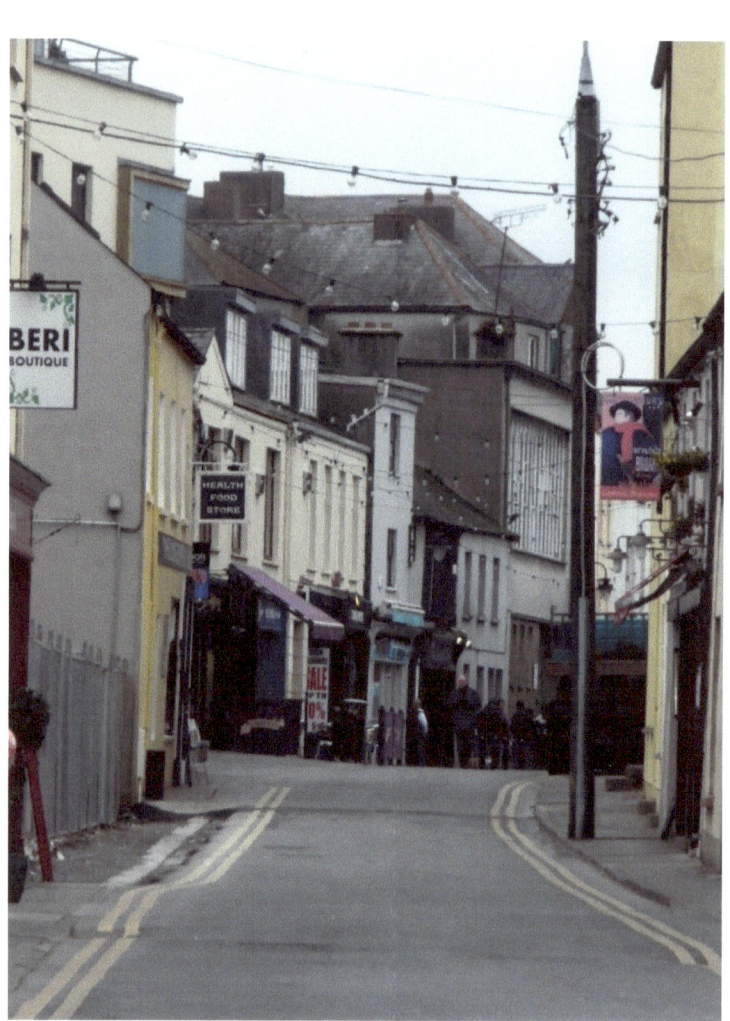

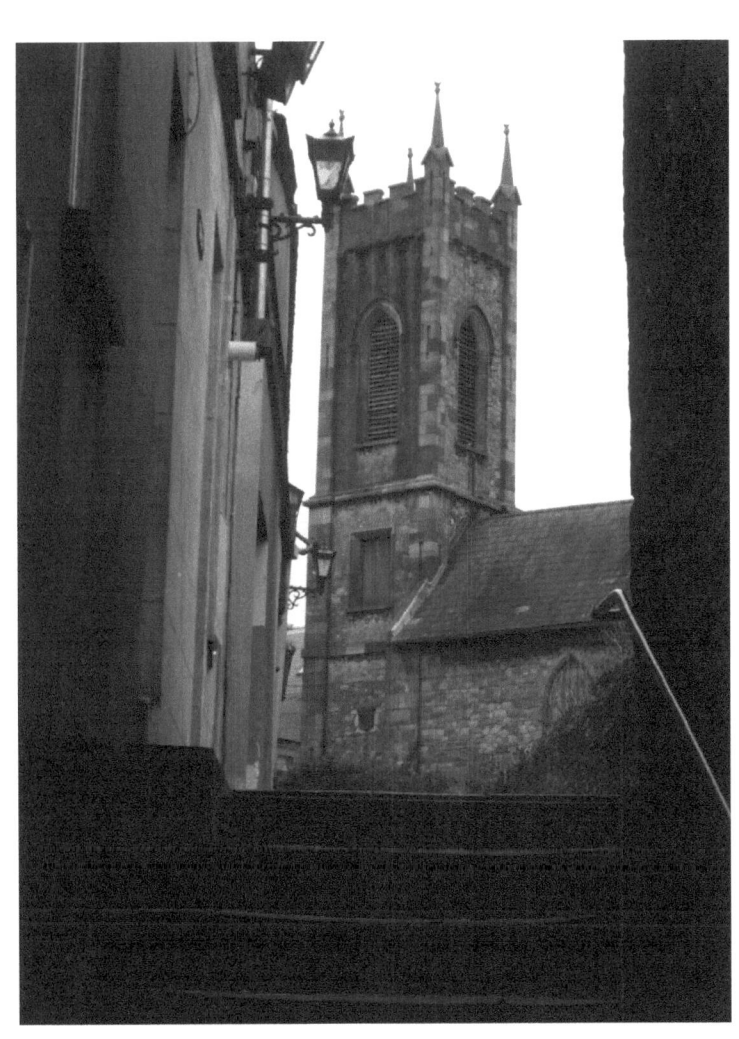

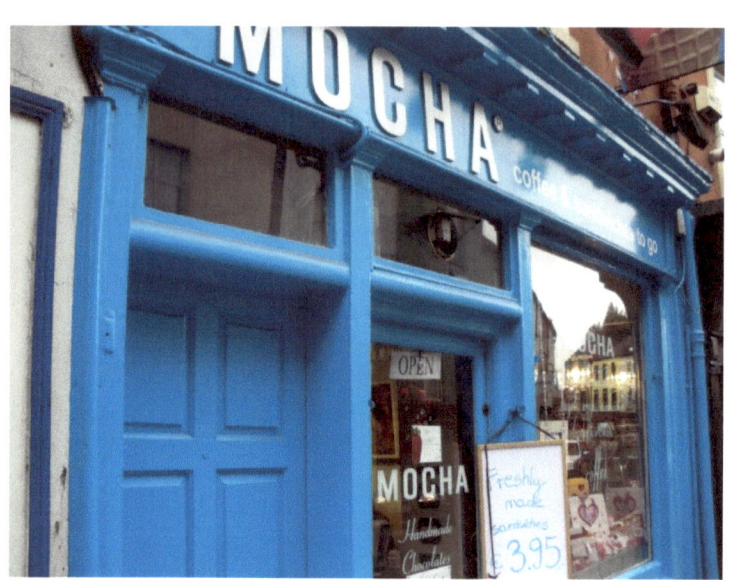

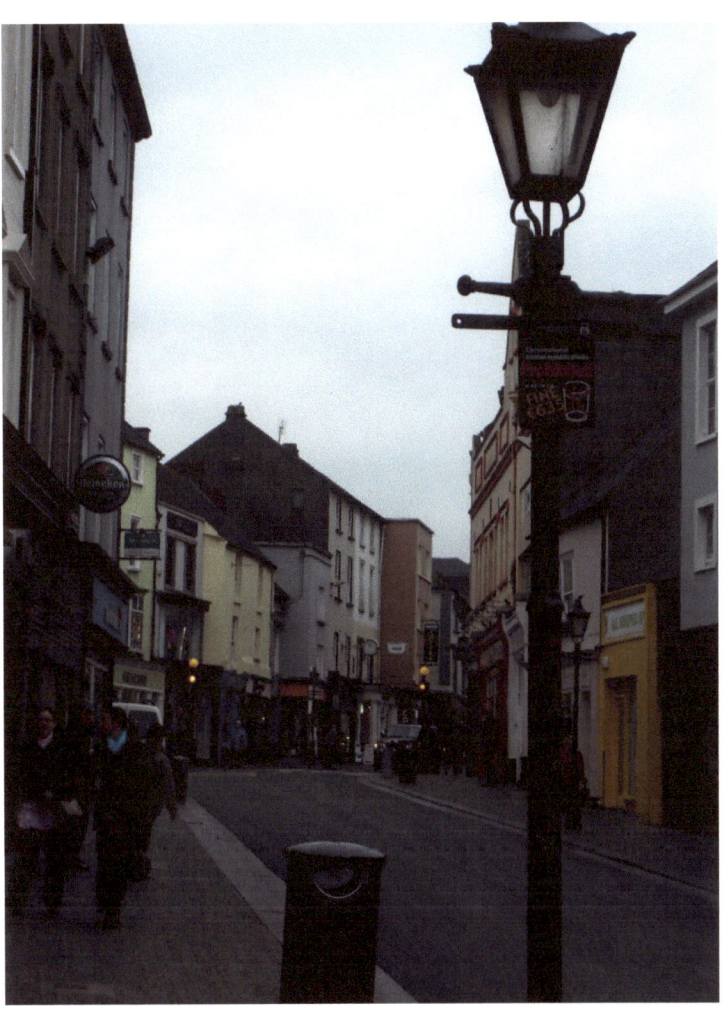

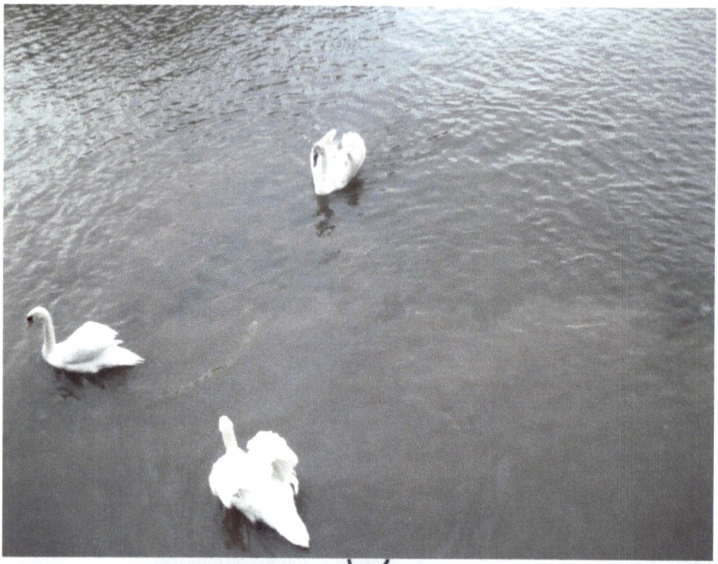

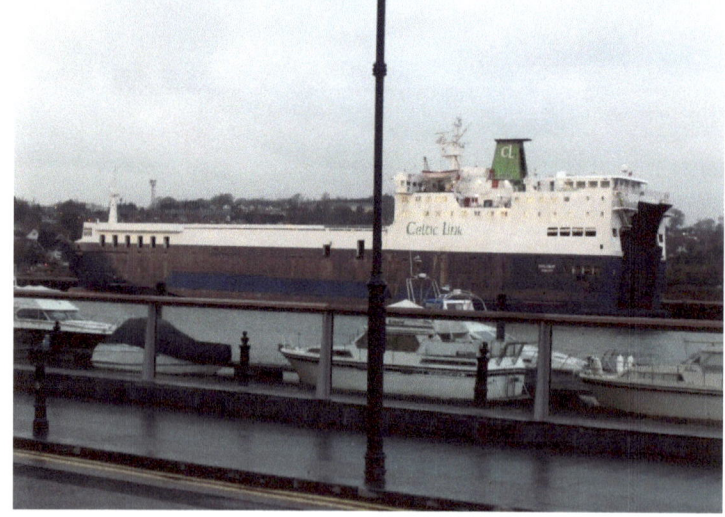

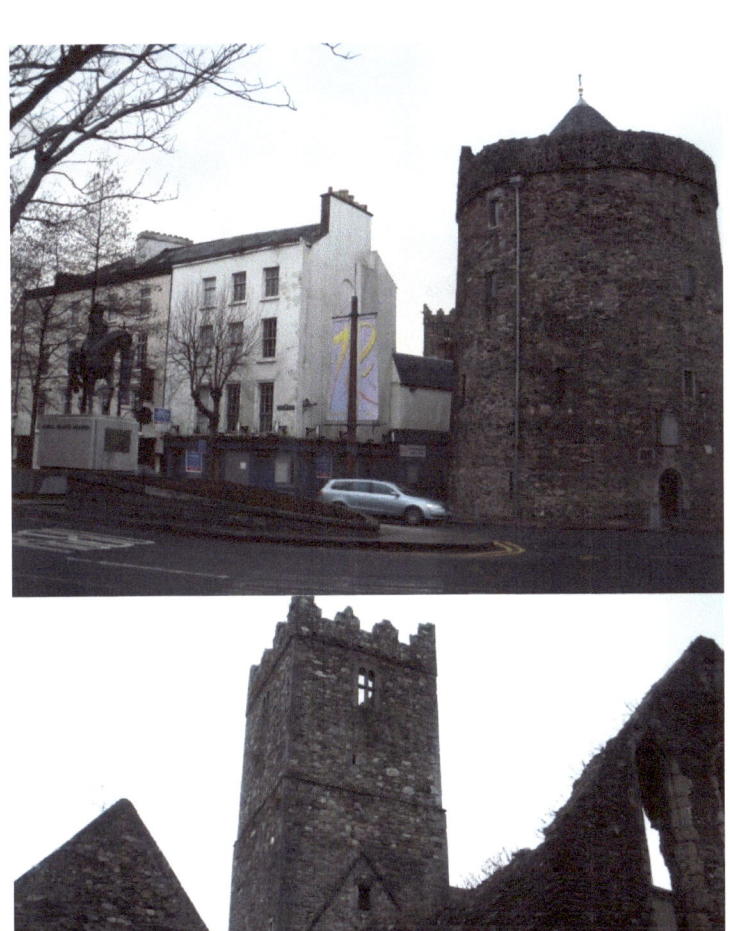

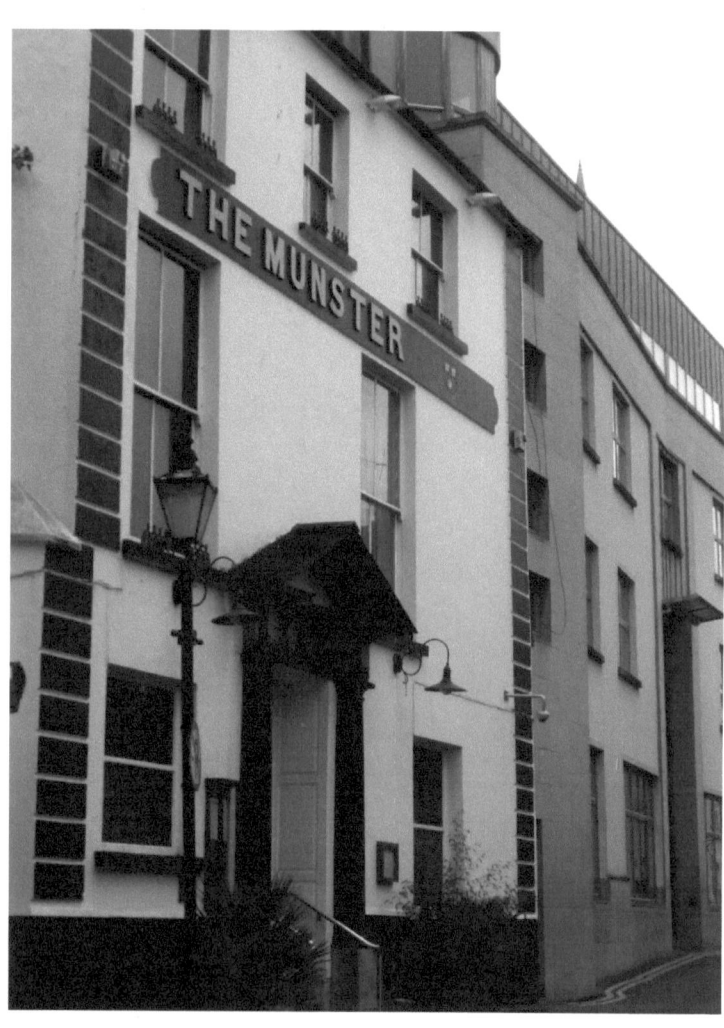

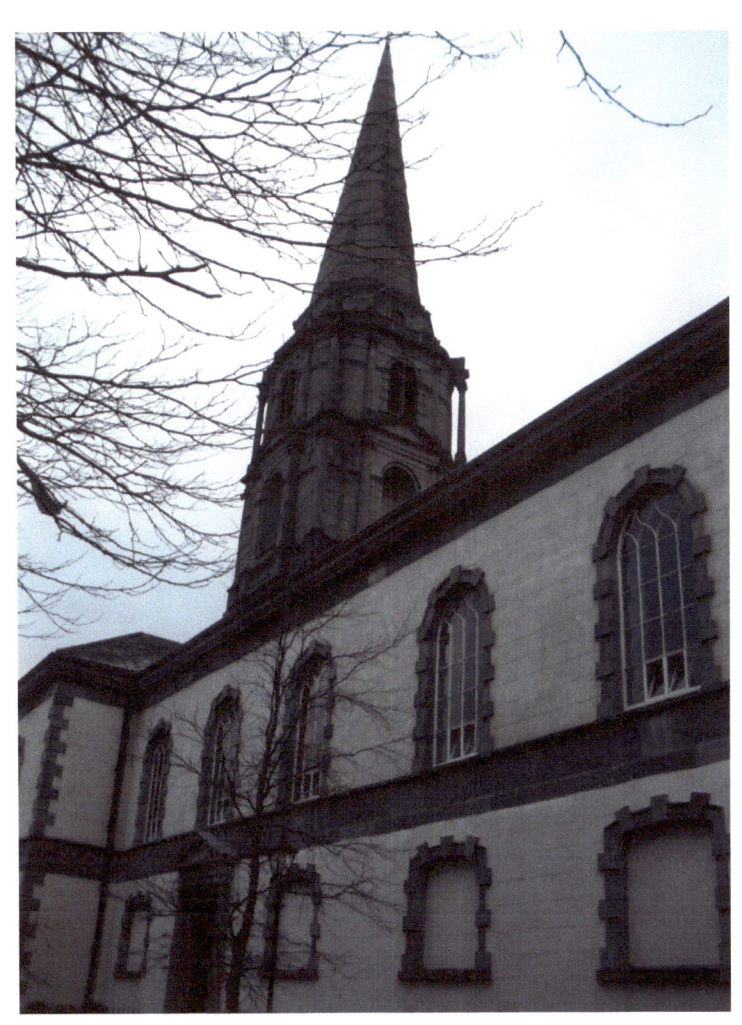

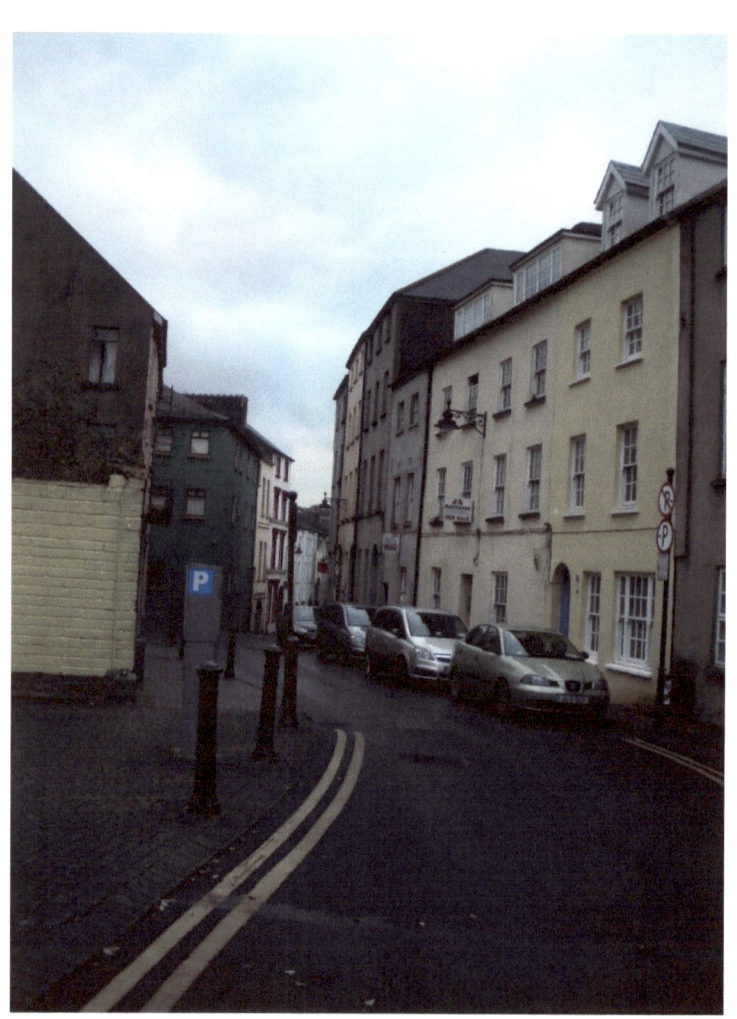

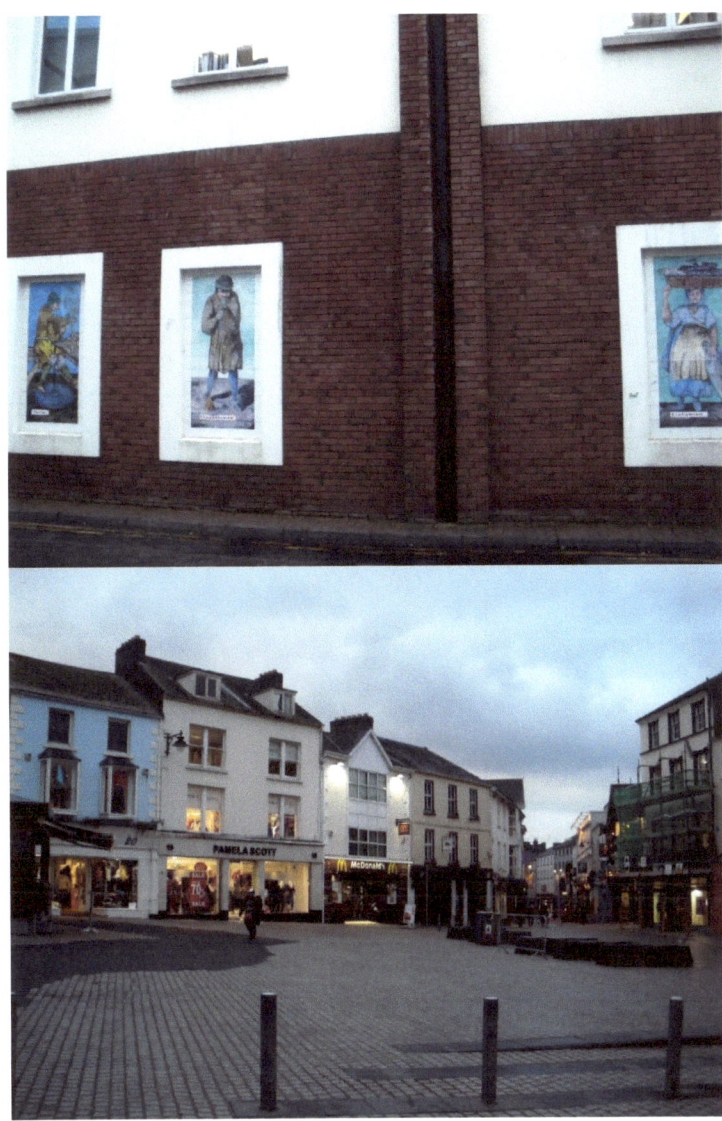

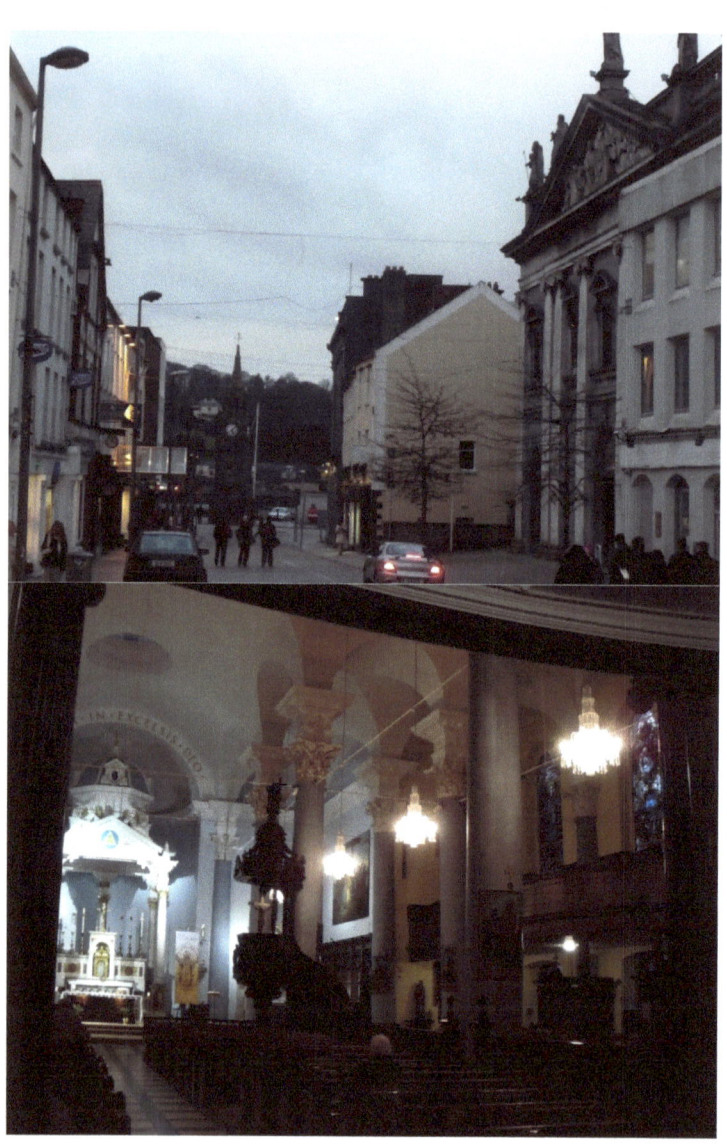

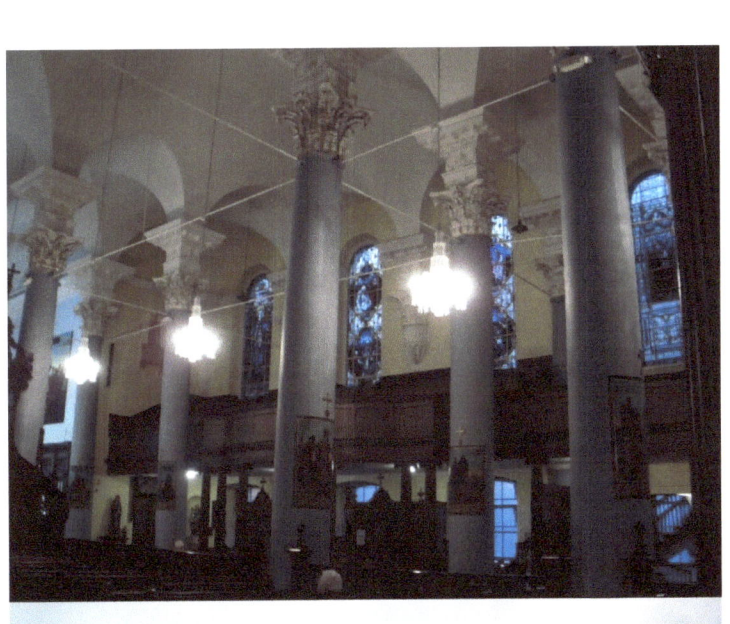

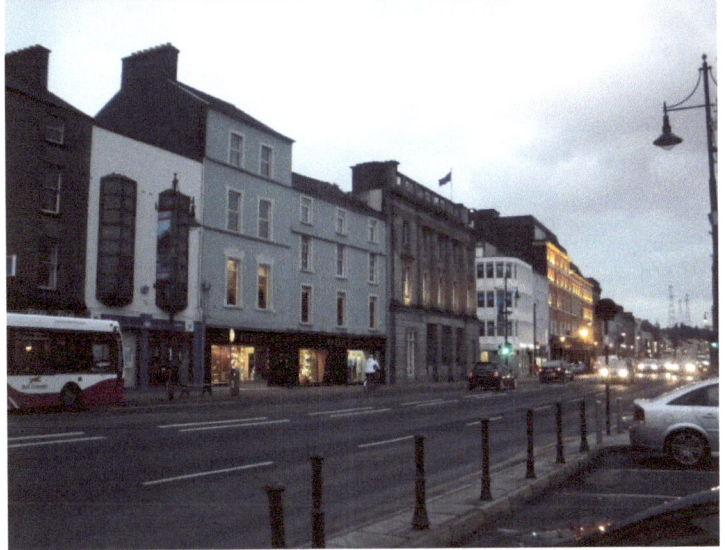

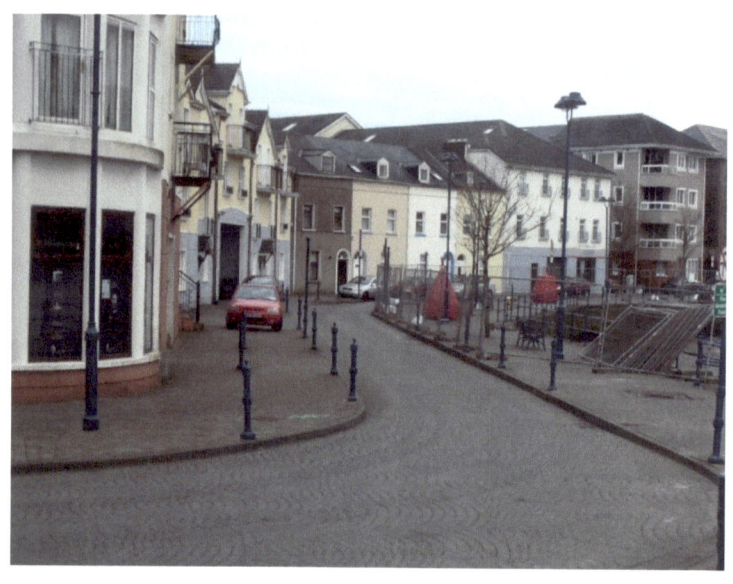

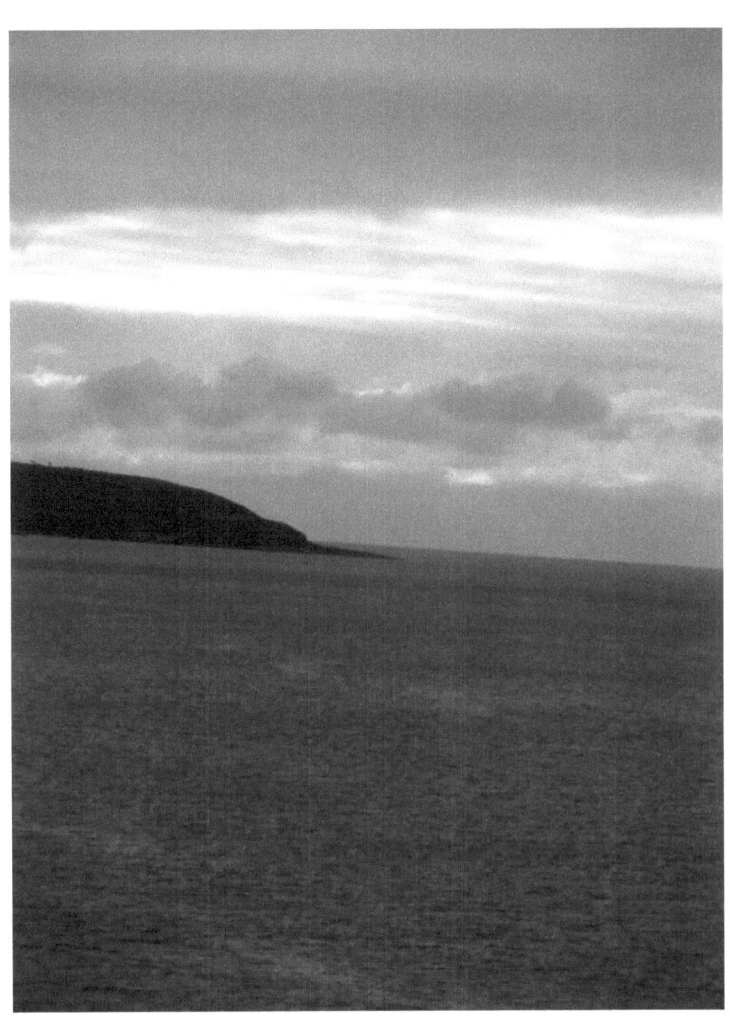

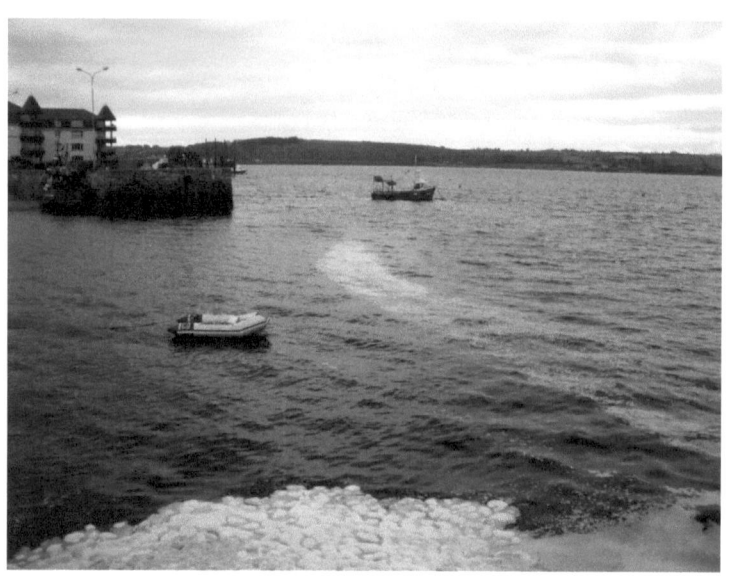

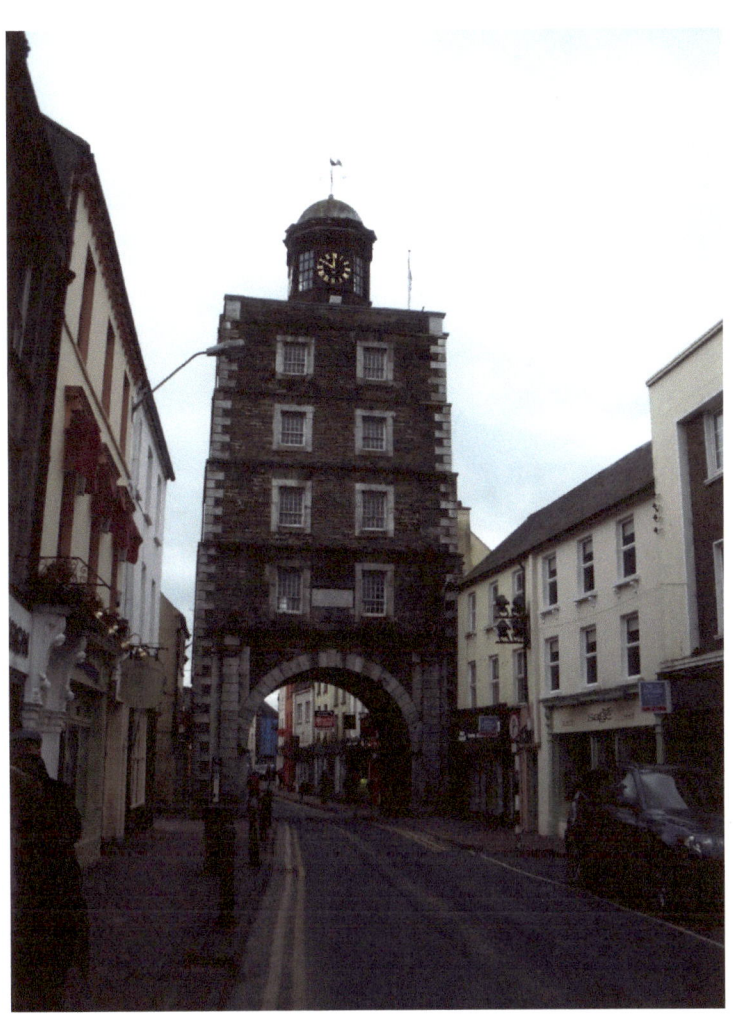

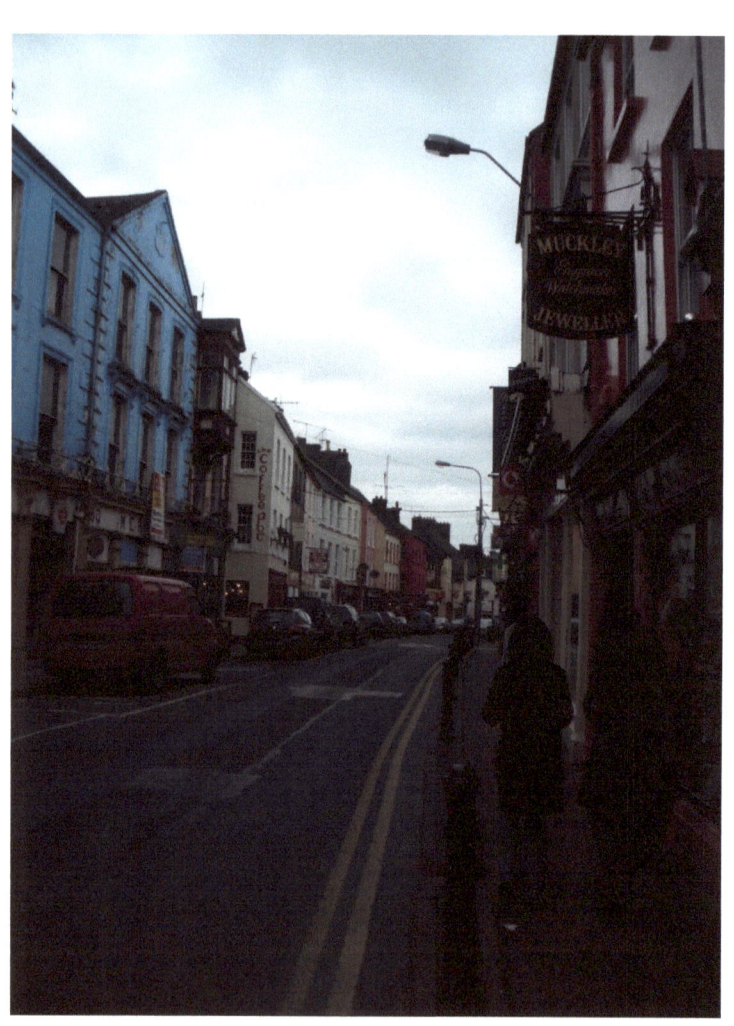

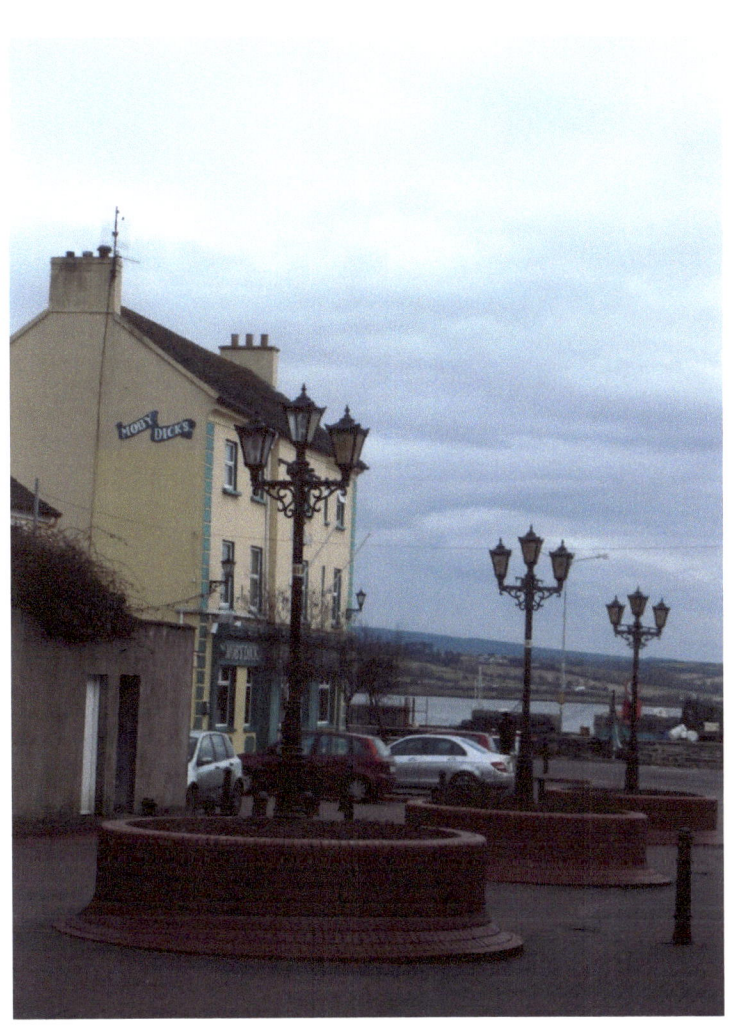

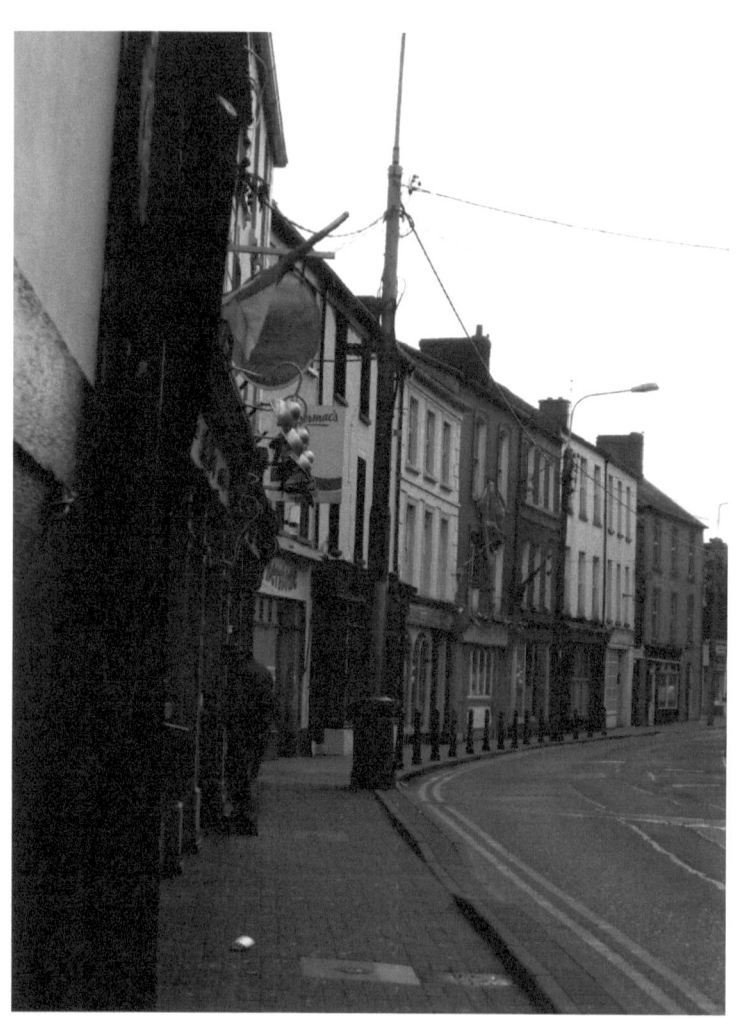

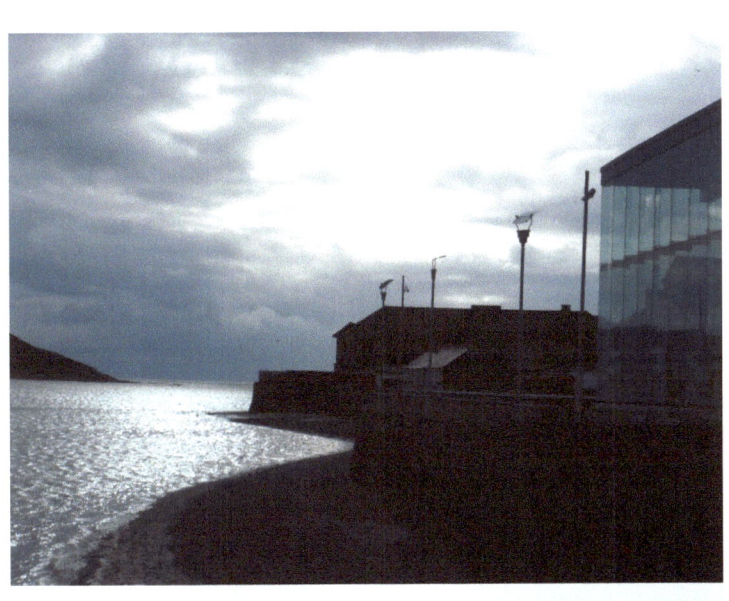

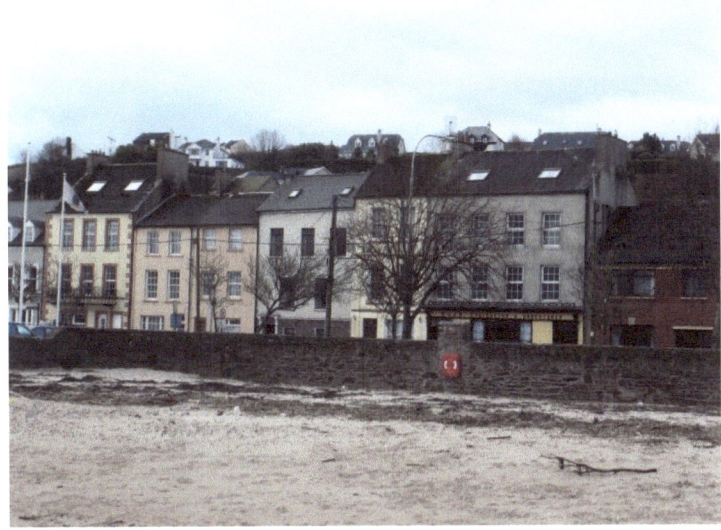

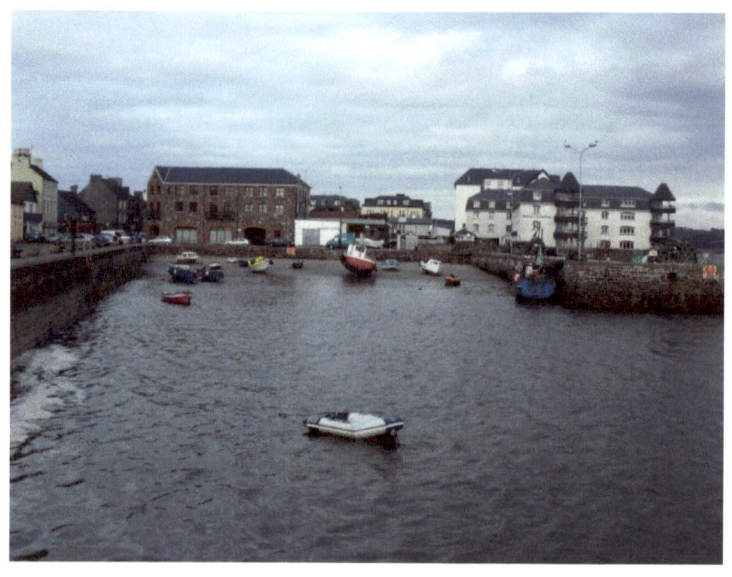

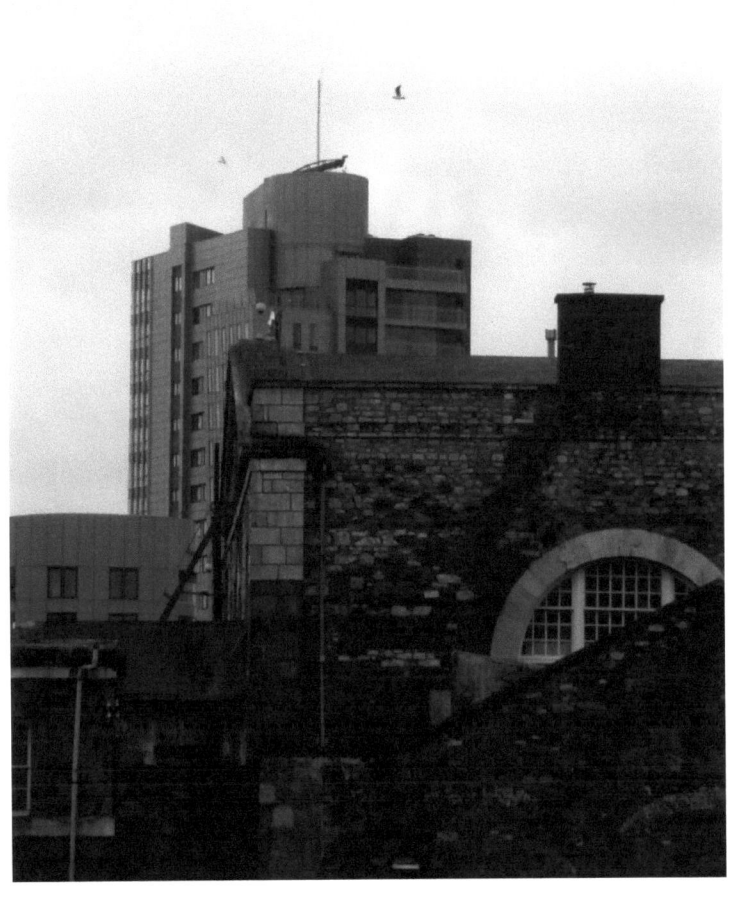

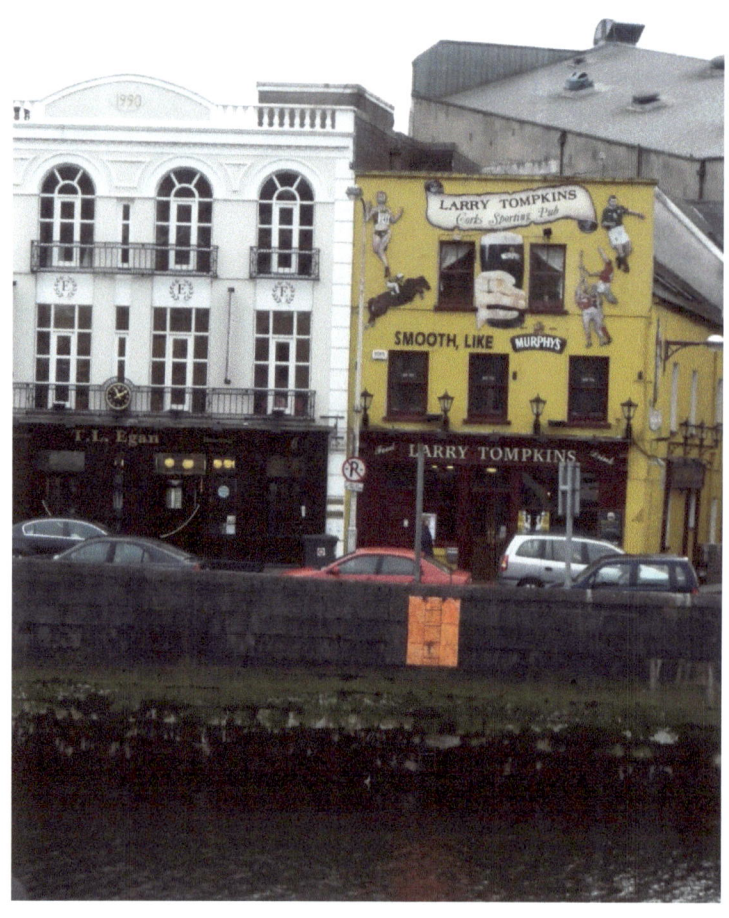

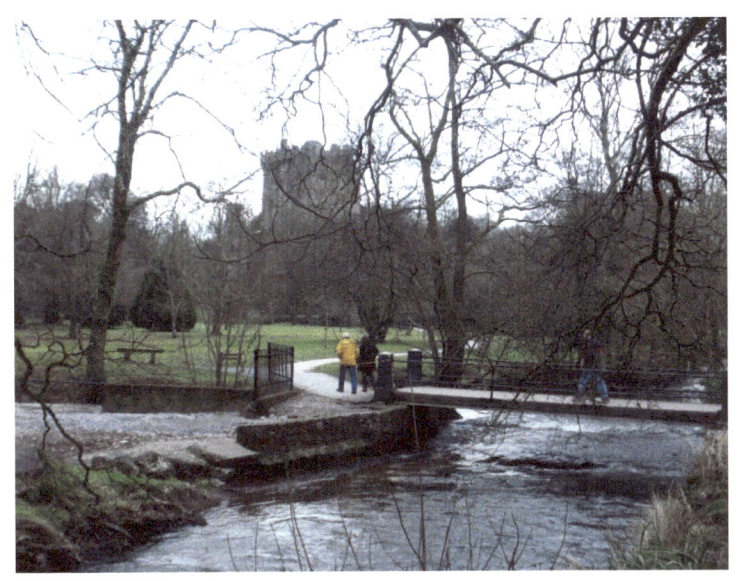

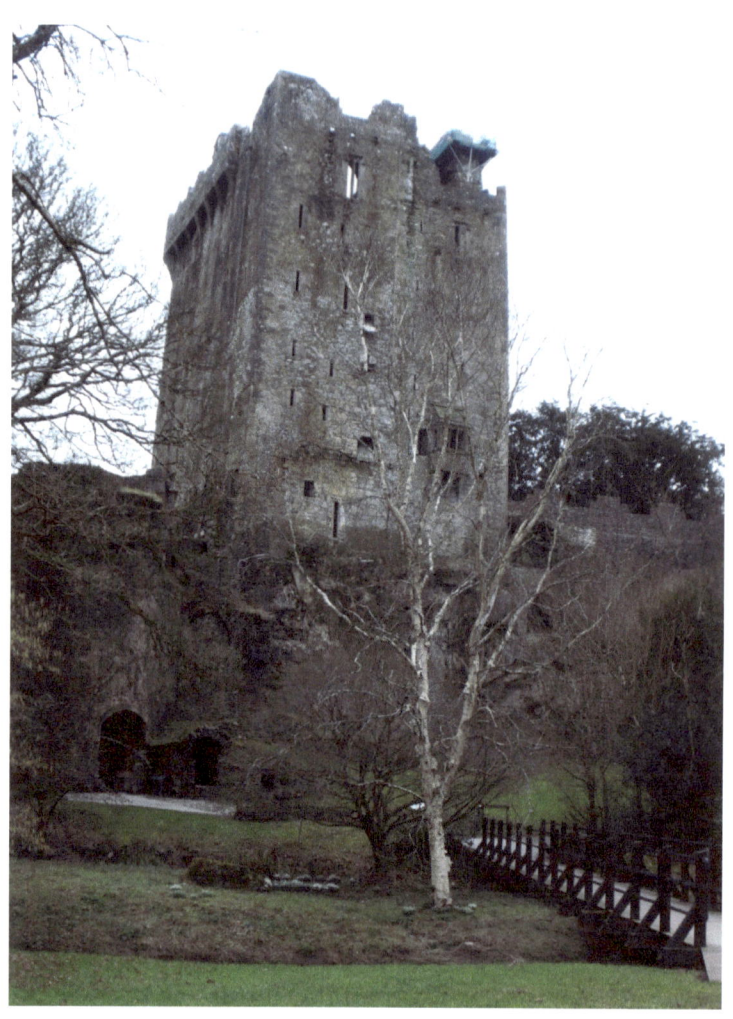

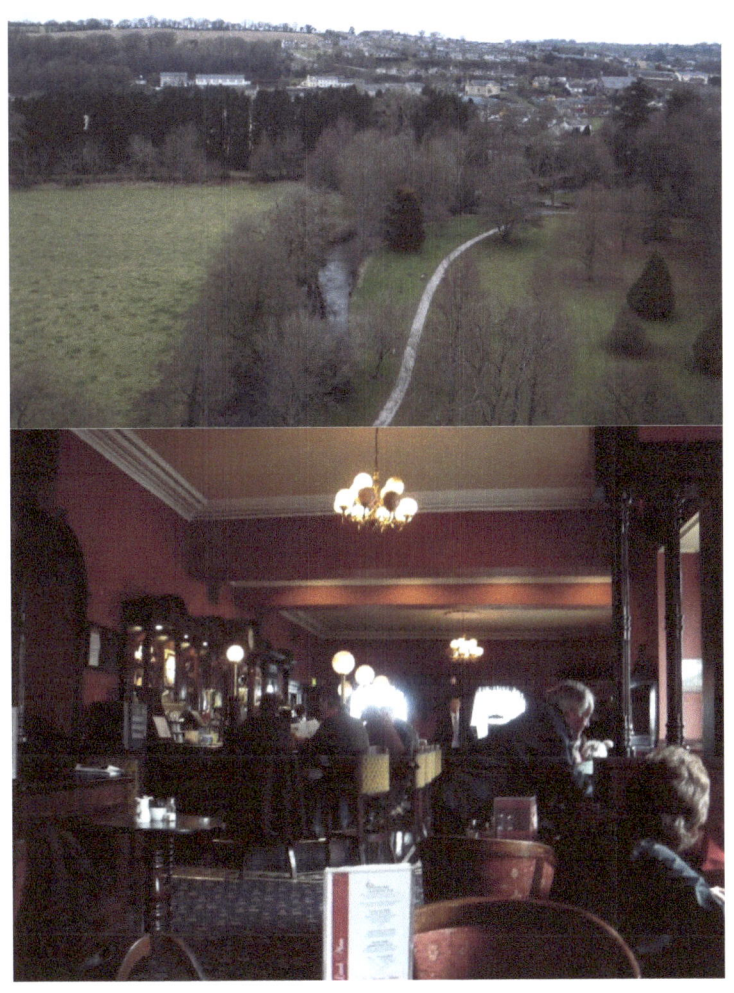

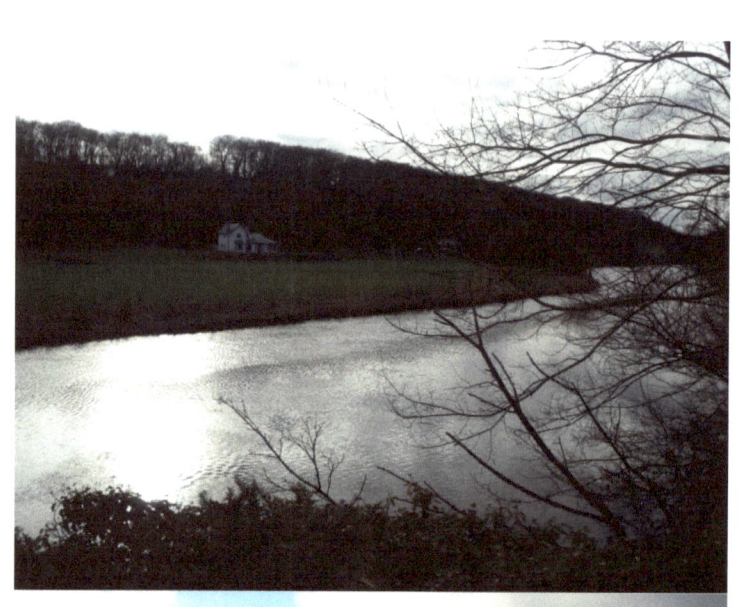

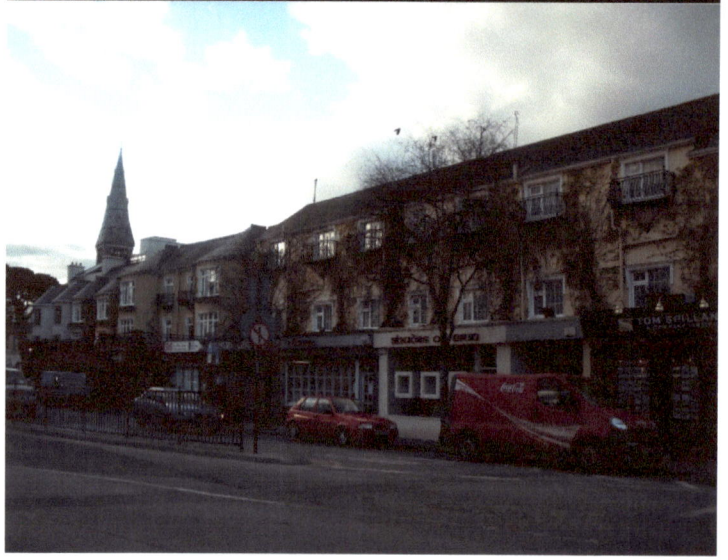

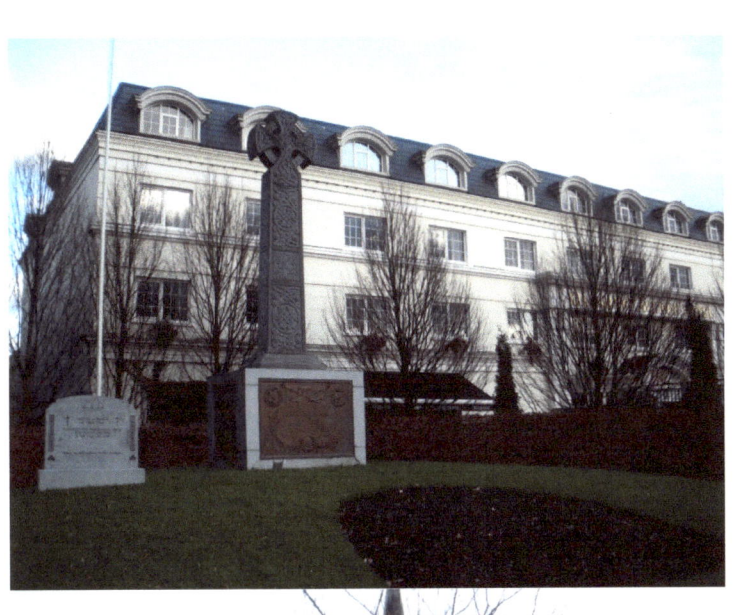

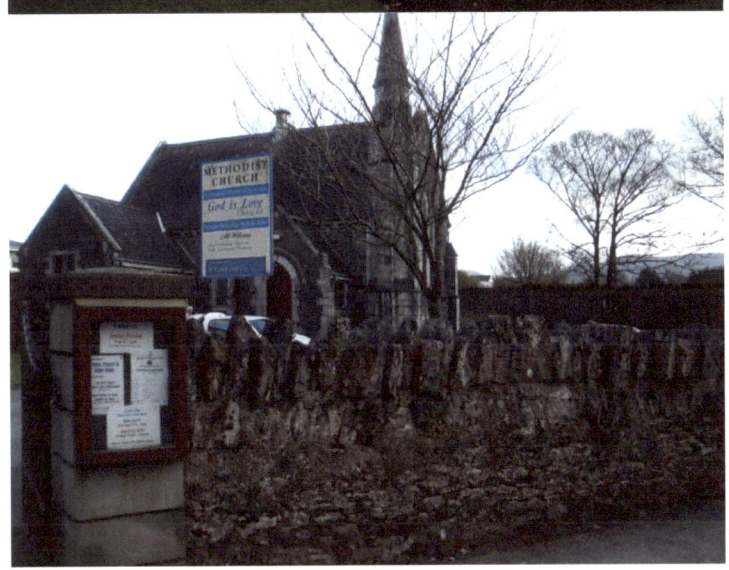

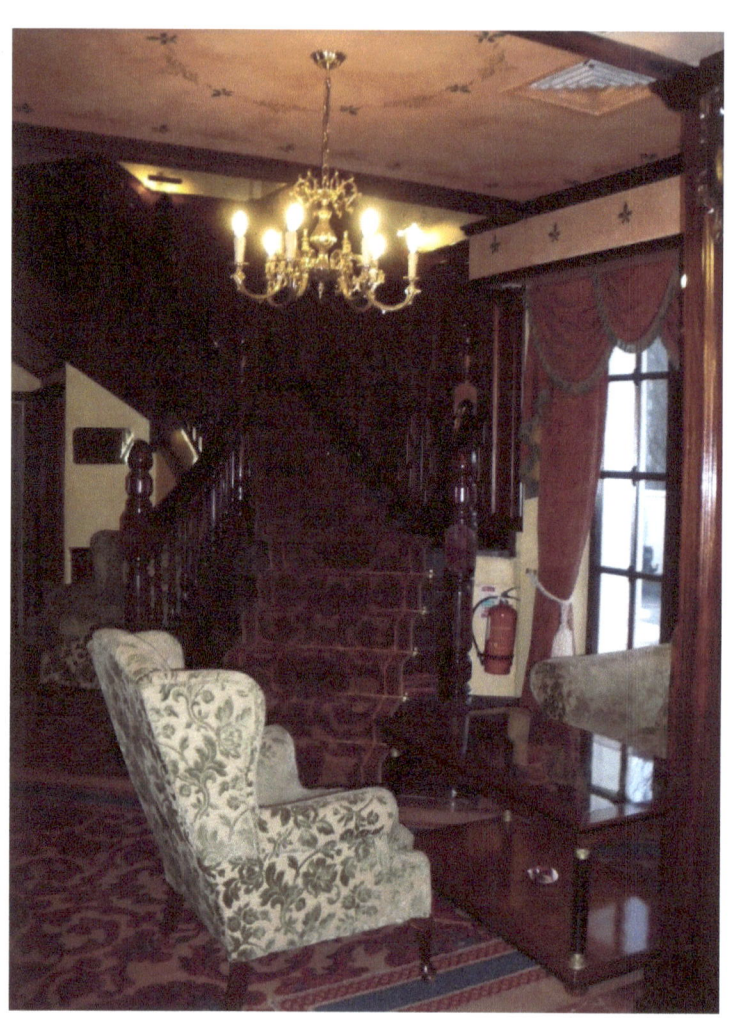

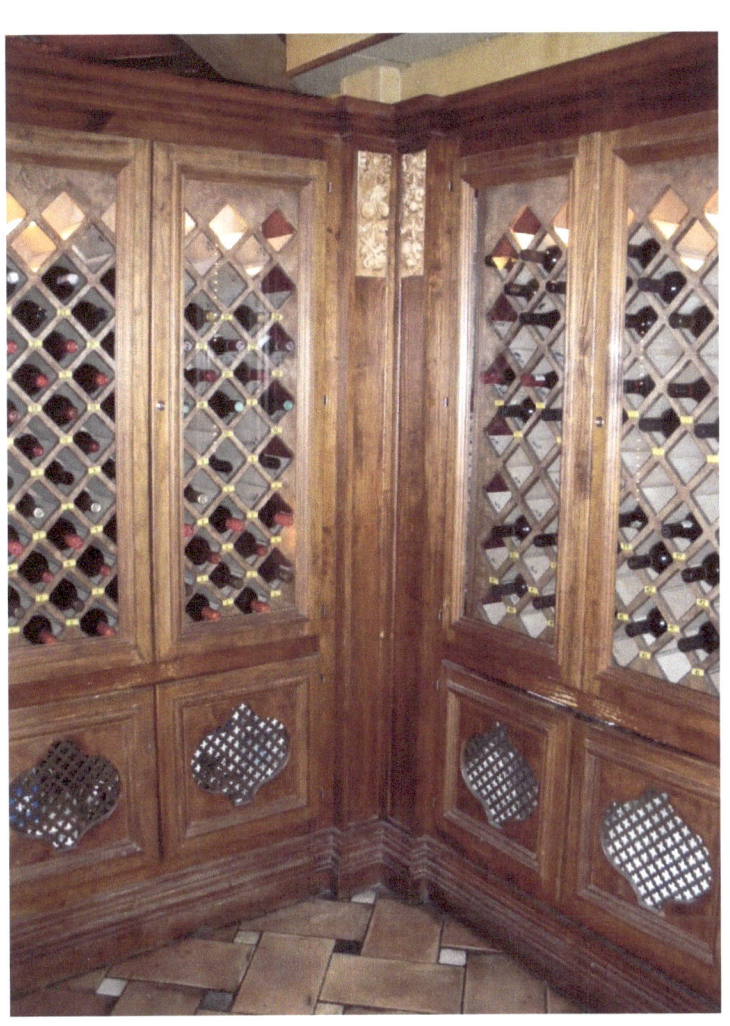

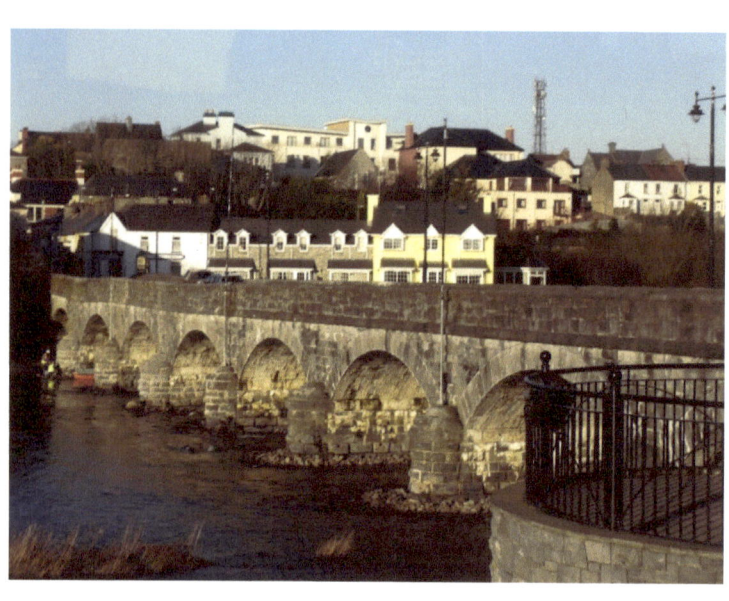

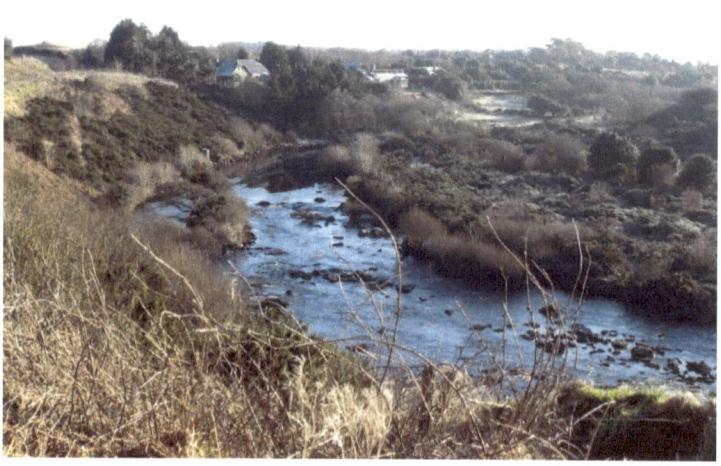

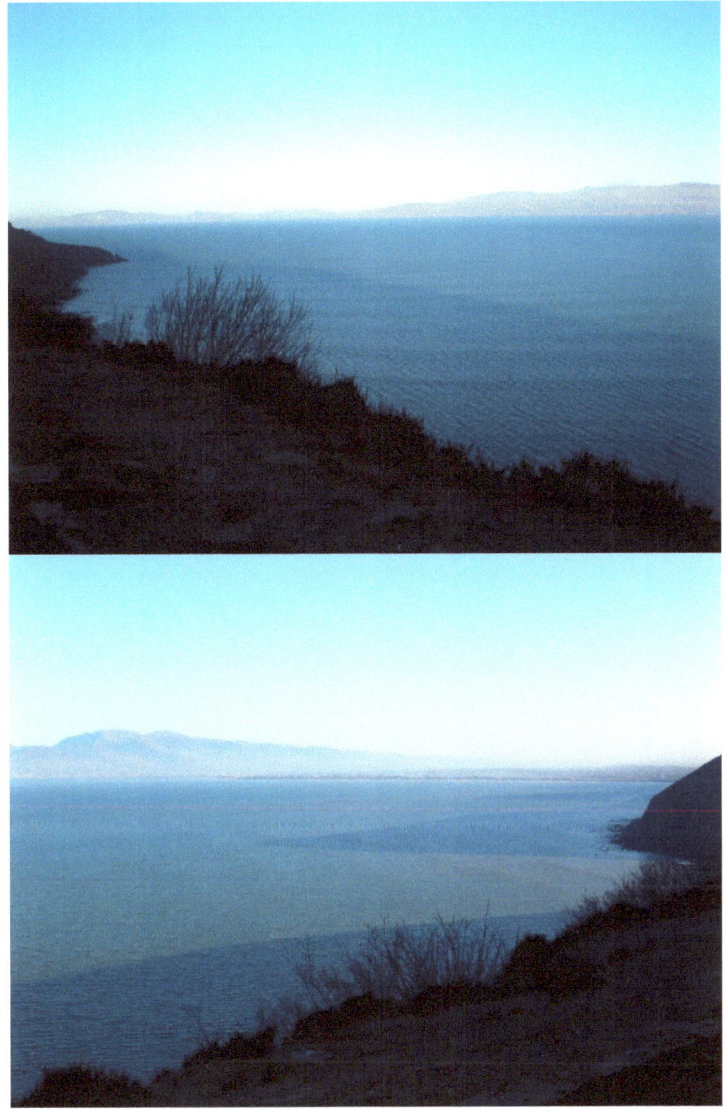

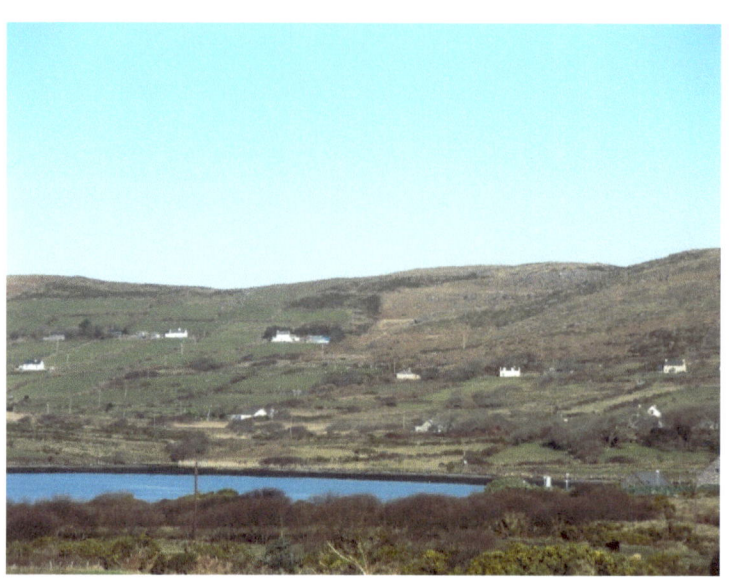

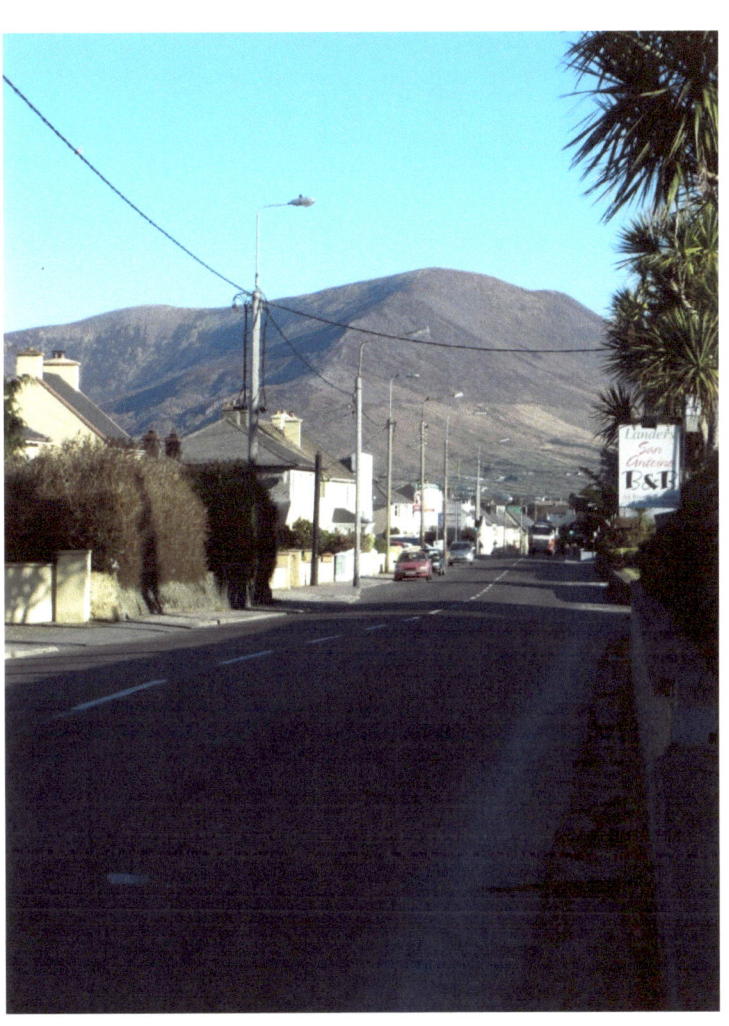

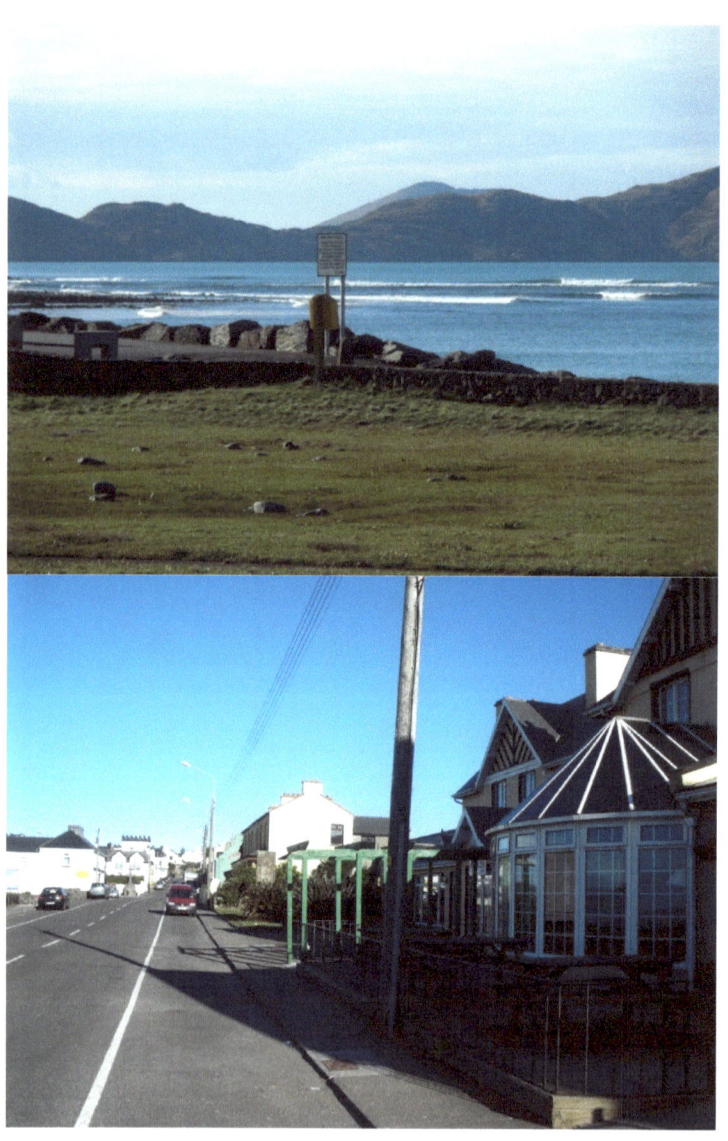

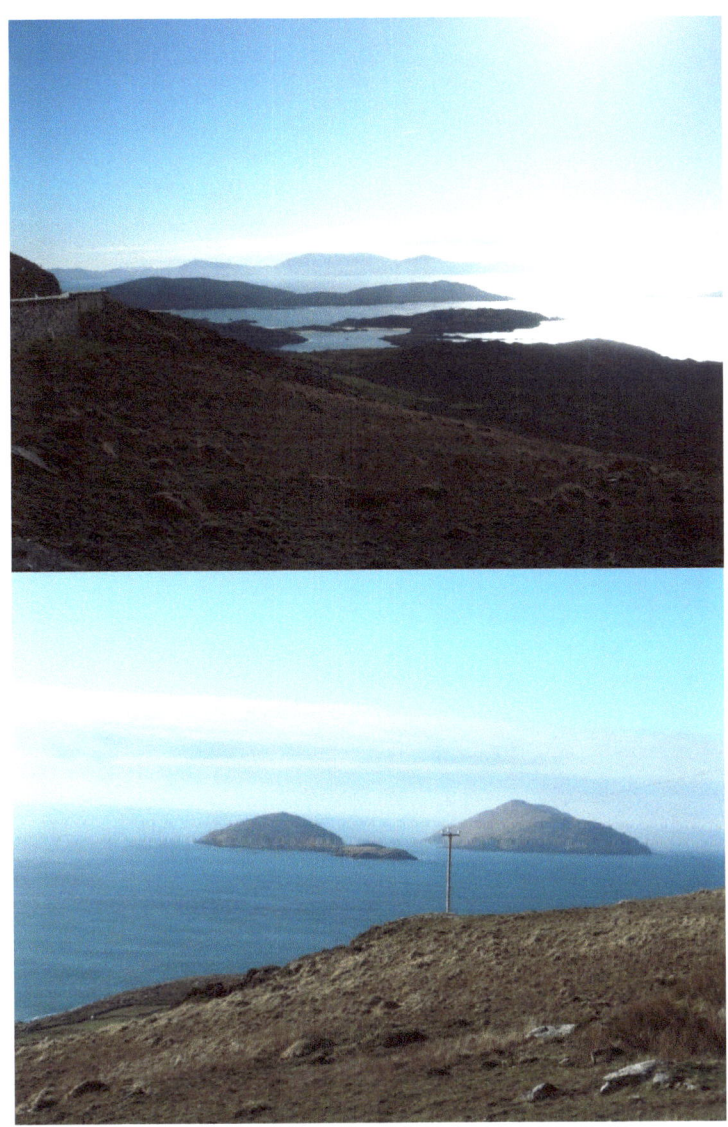

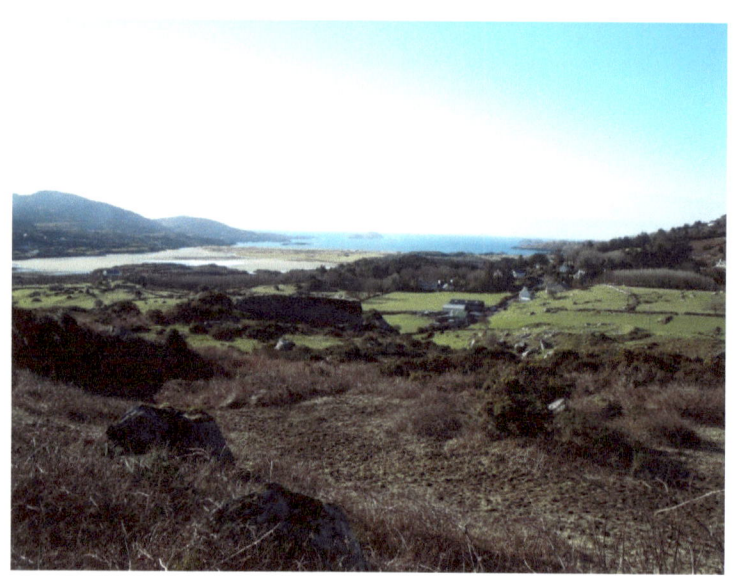

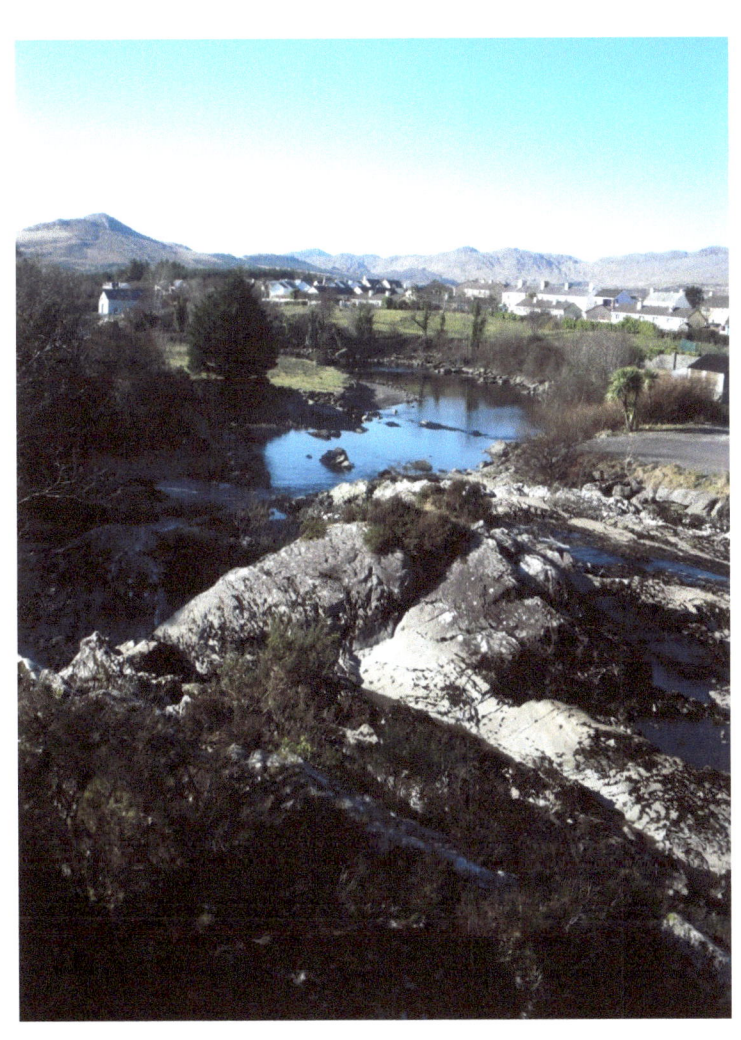

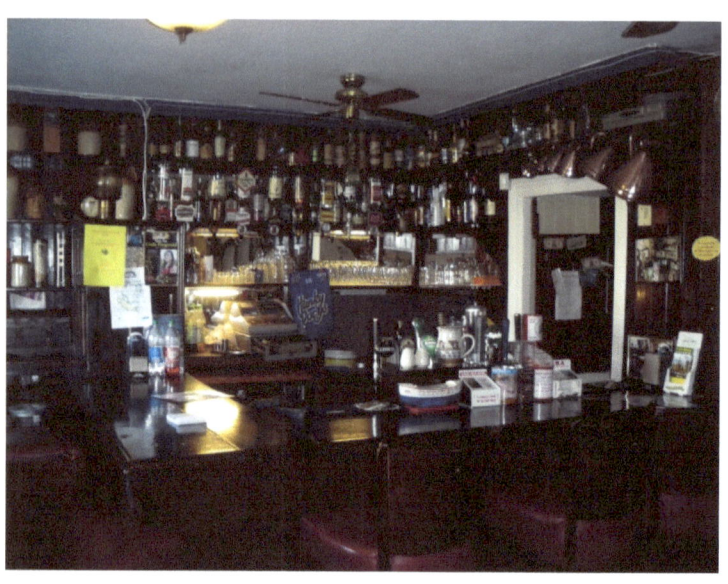

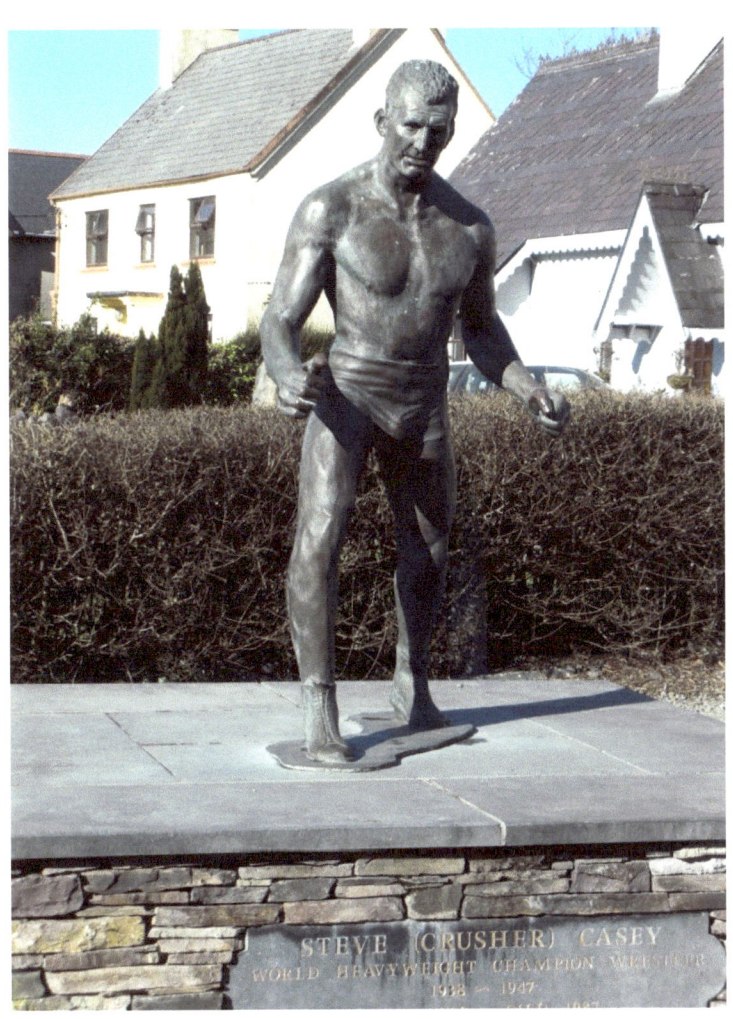

STEVE (CRUSHER) CASEY
WORLD HEAVYWEIGHT CHAMPION WRESTLER
1938 — 1947

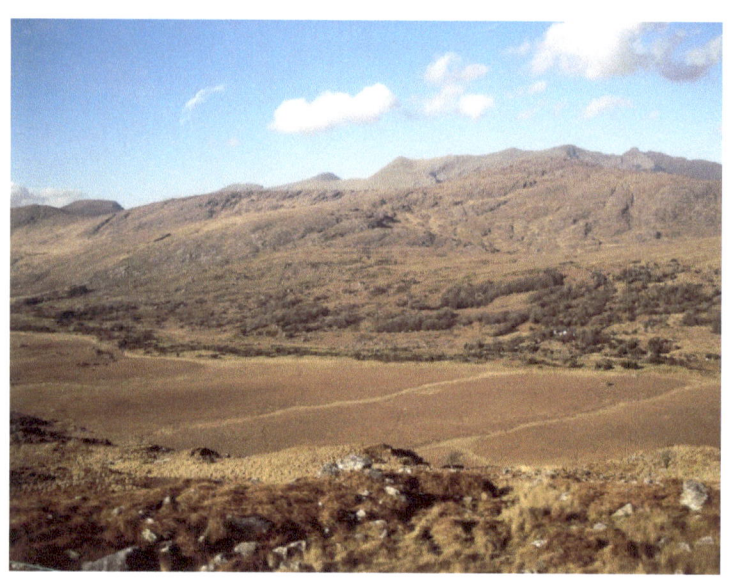

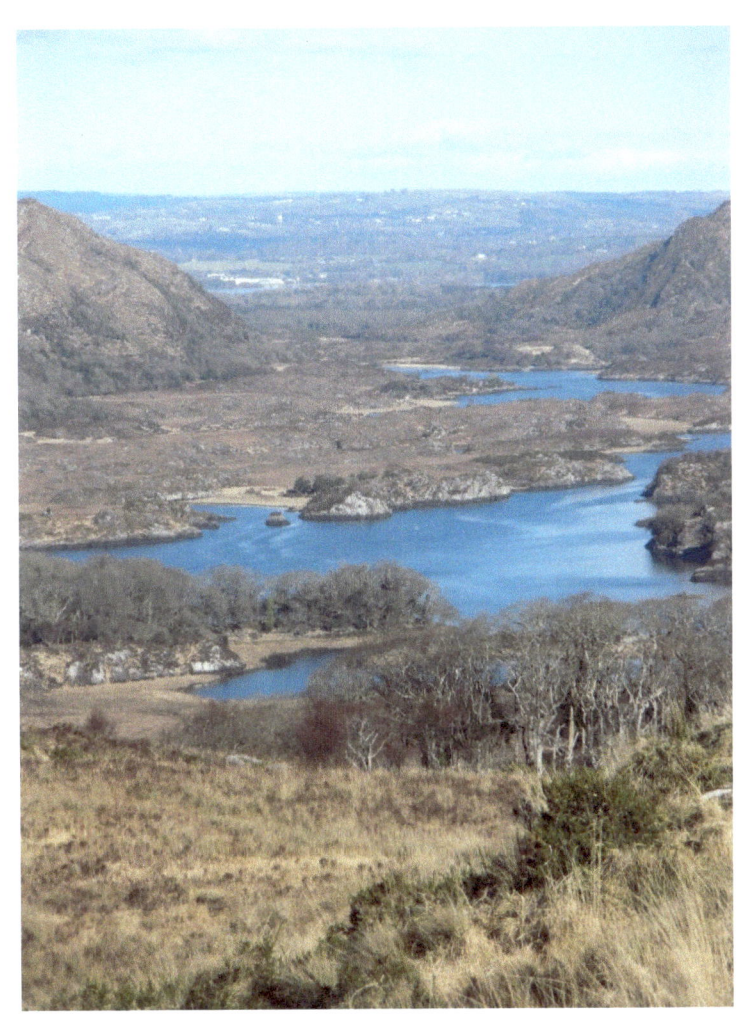

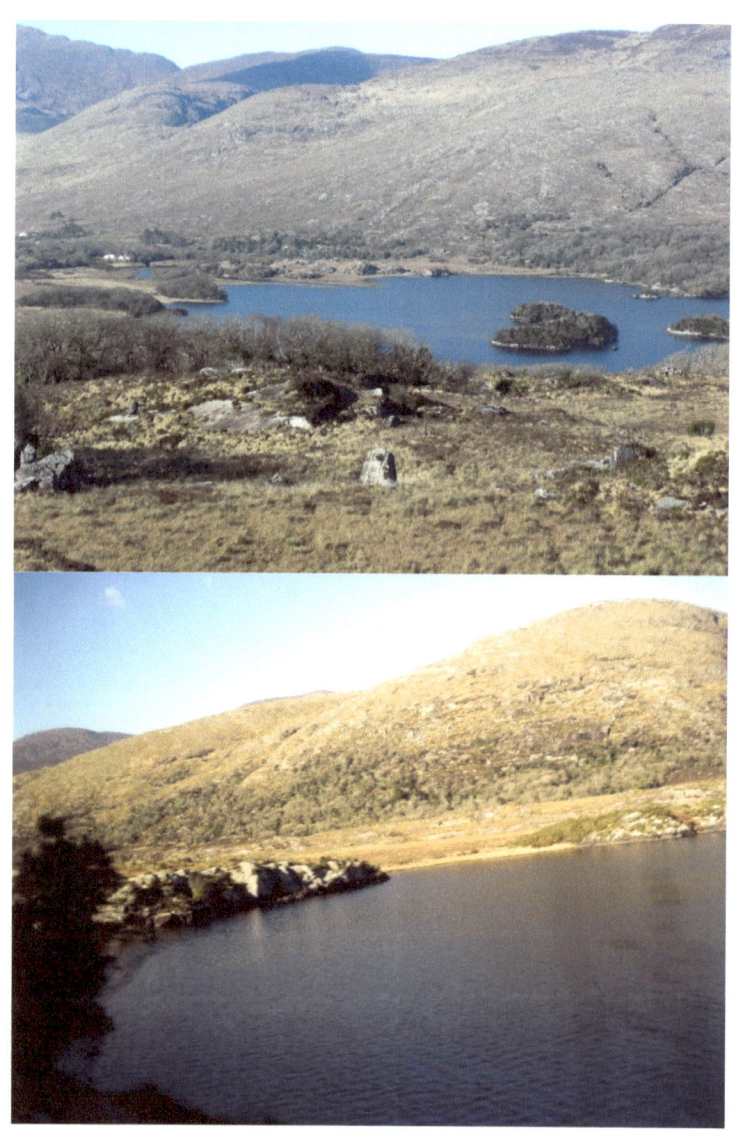

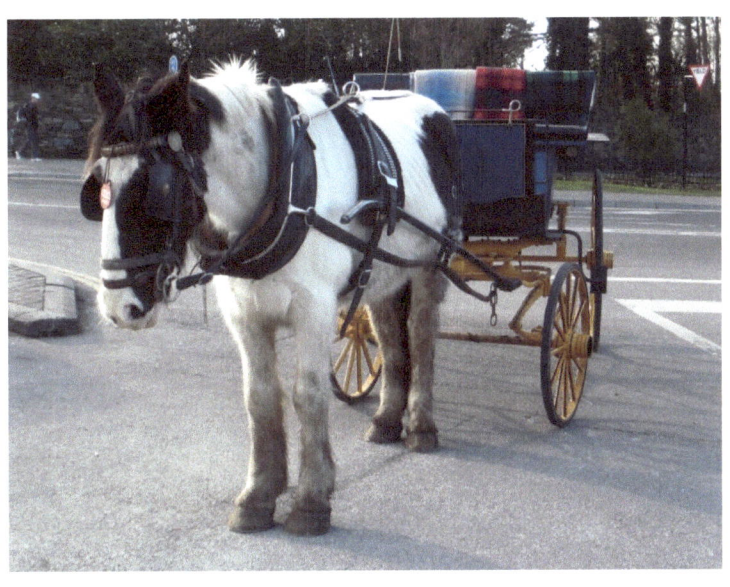

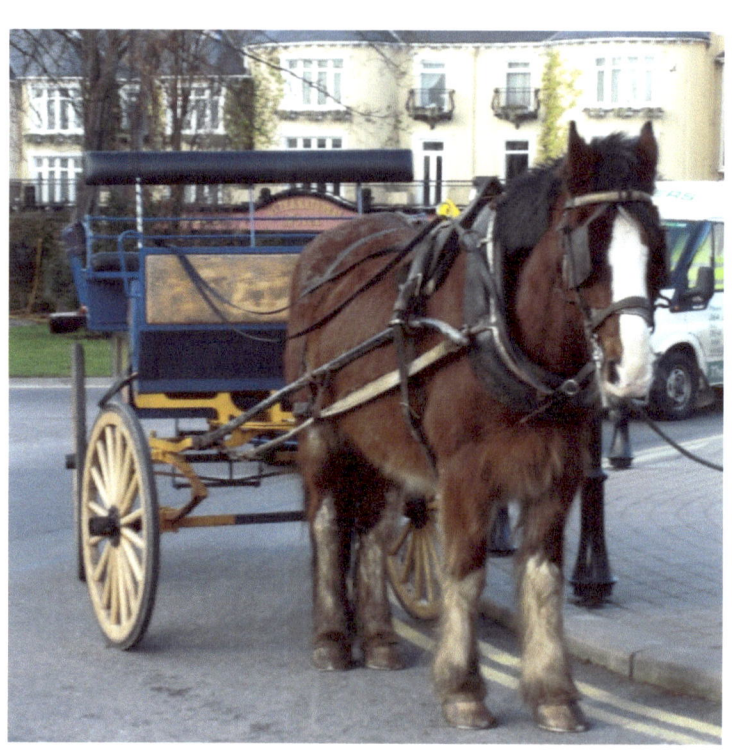

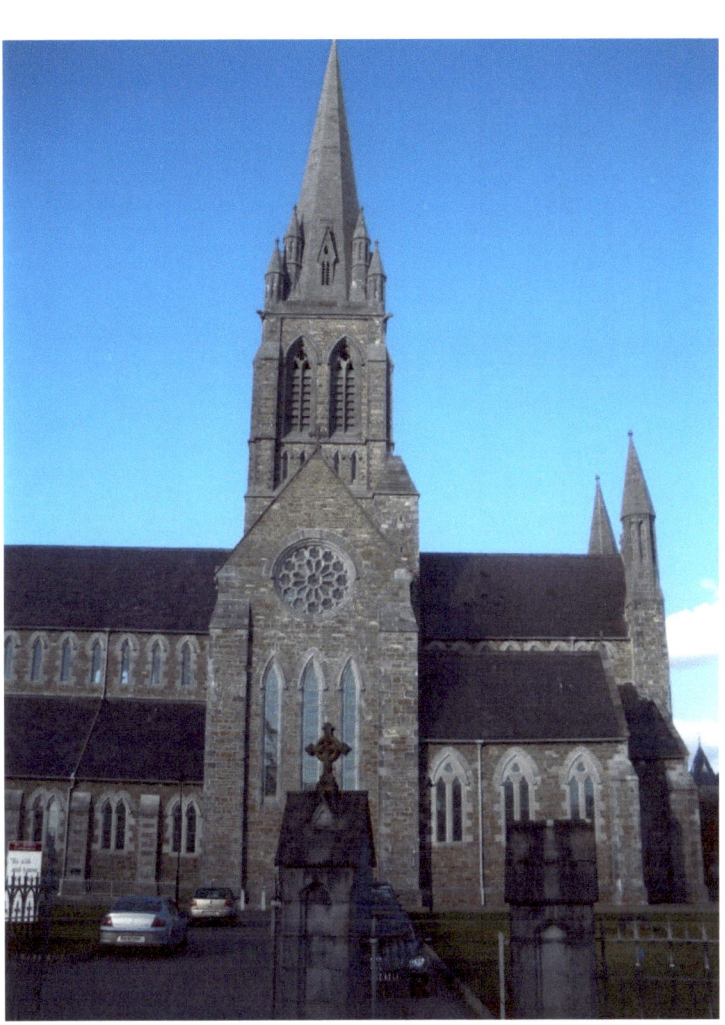

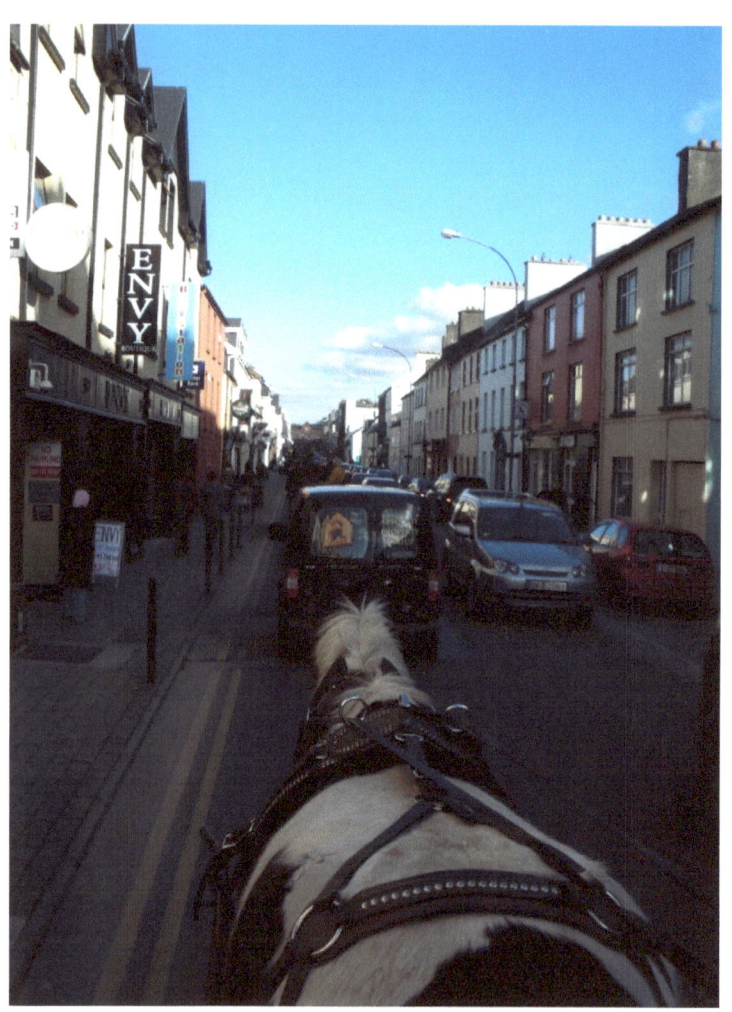

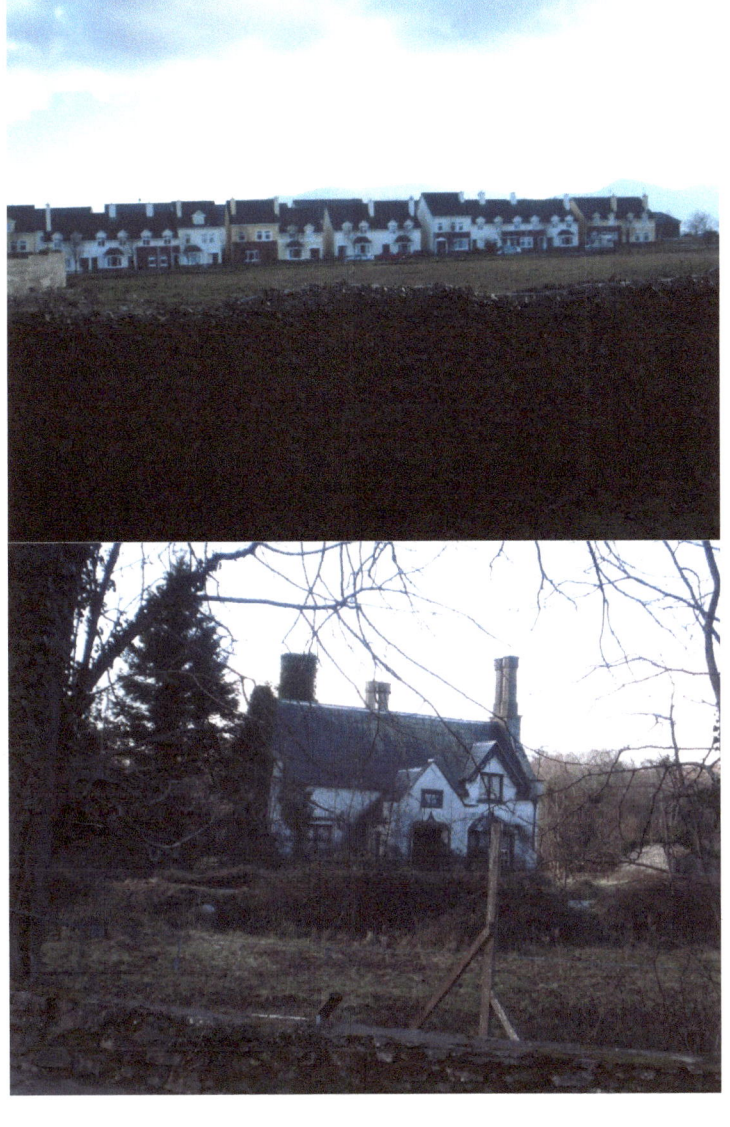

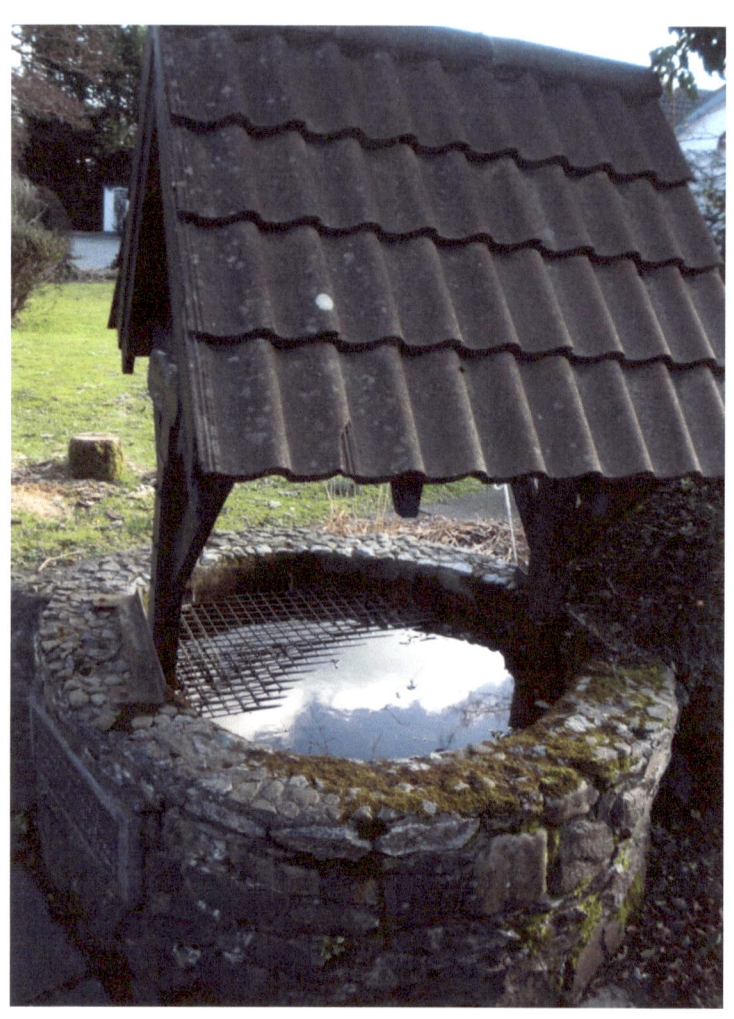

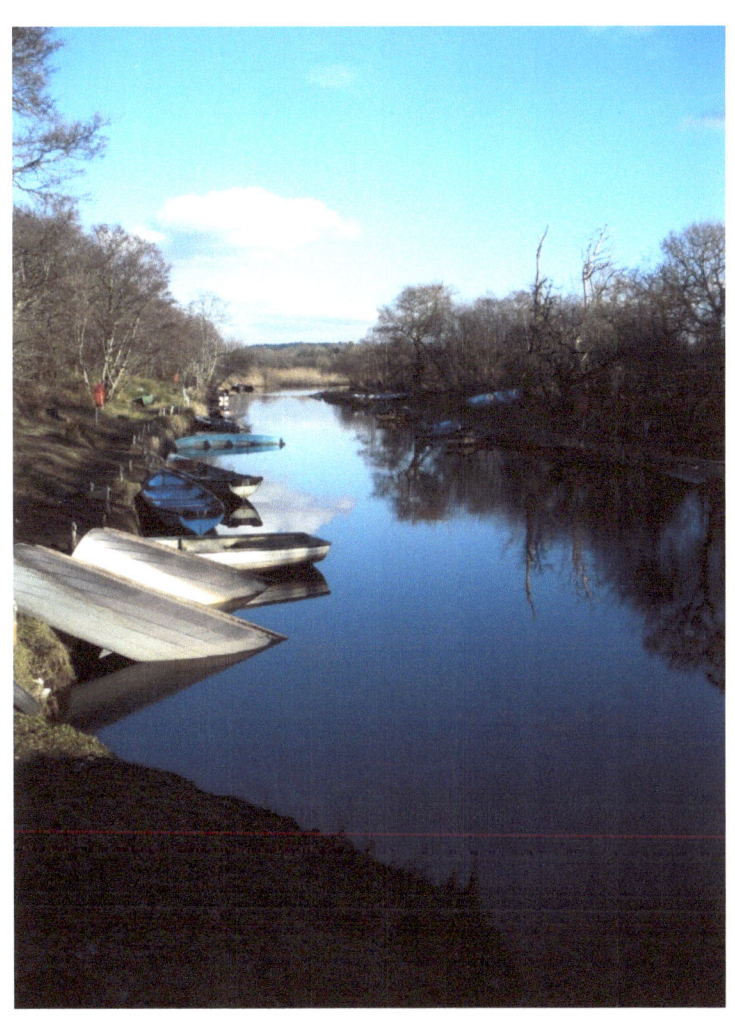

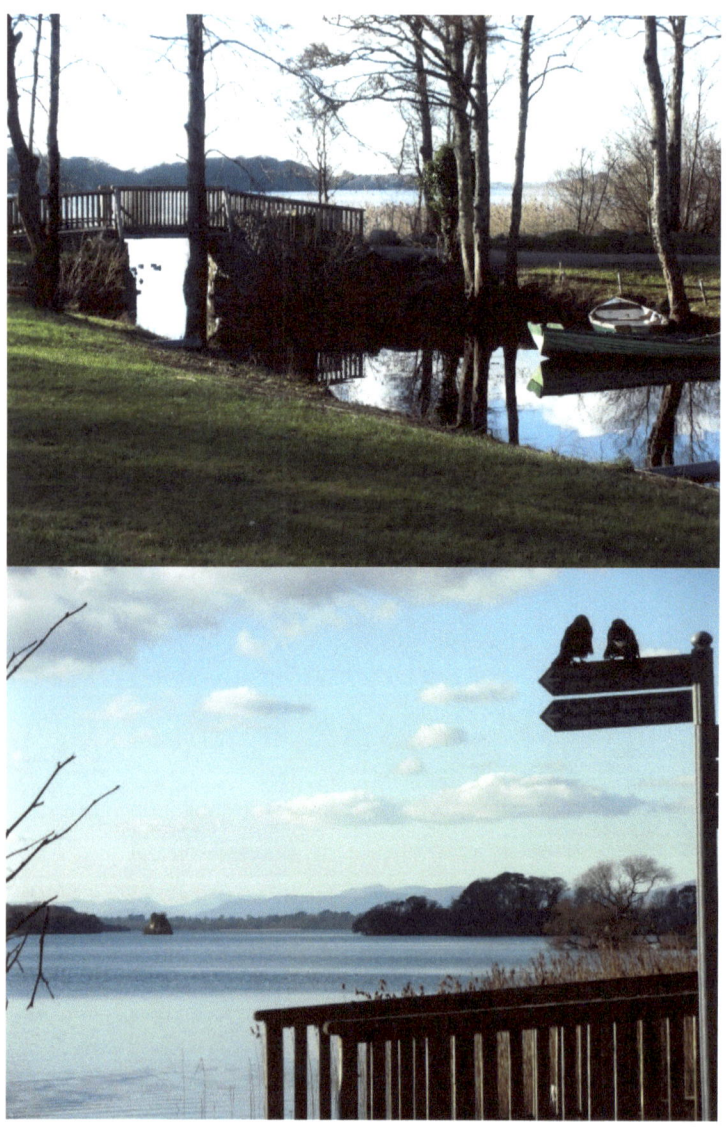

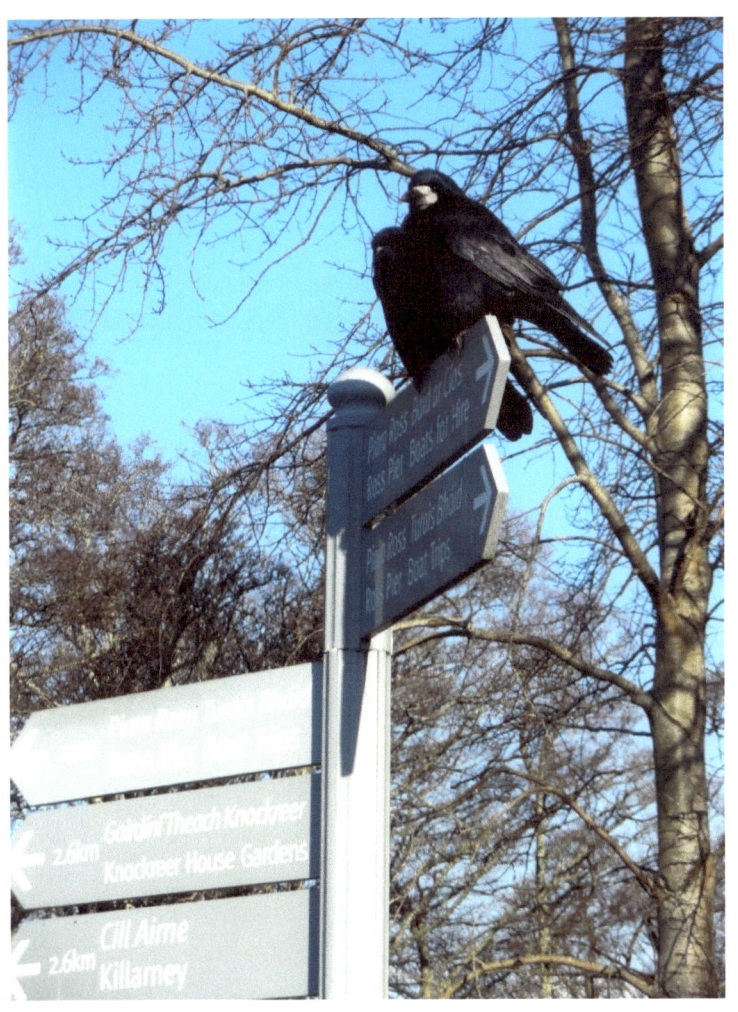

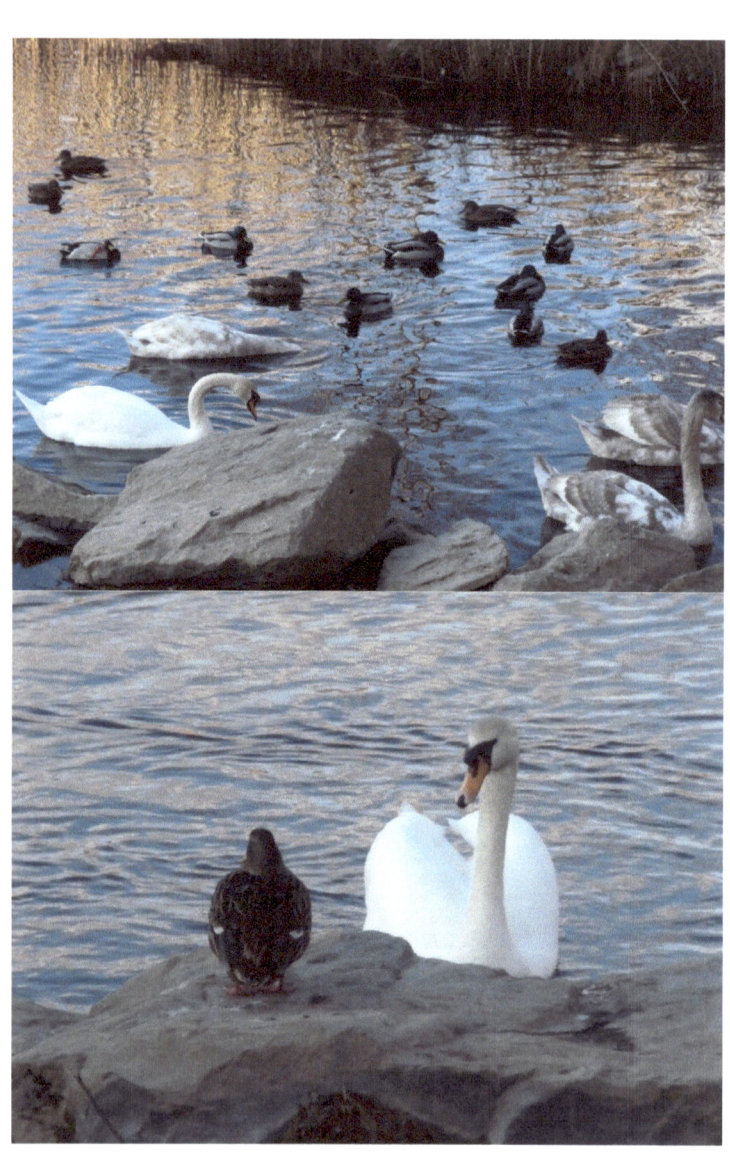

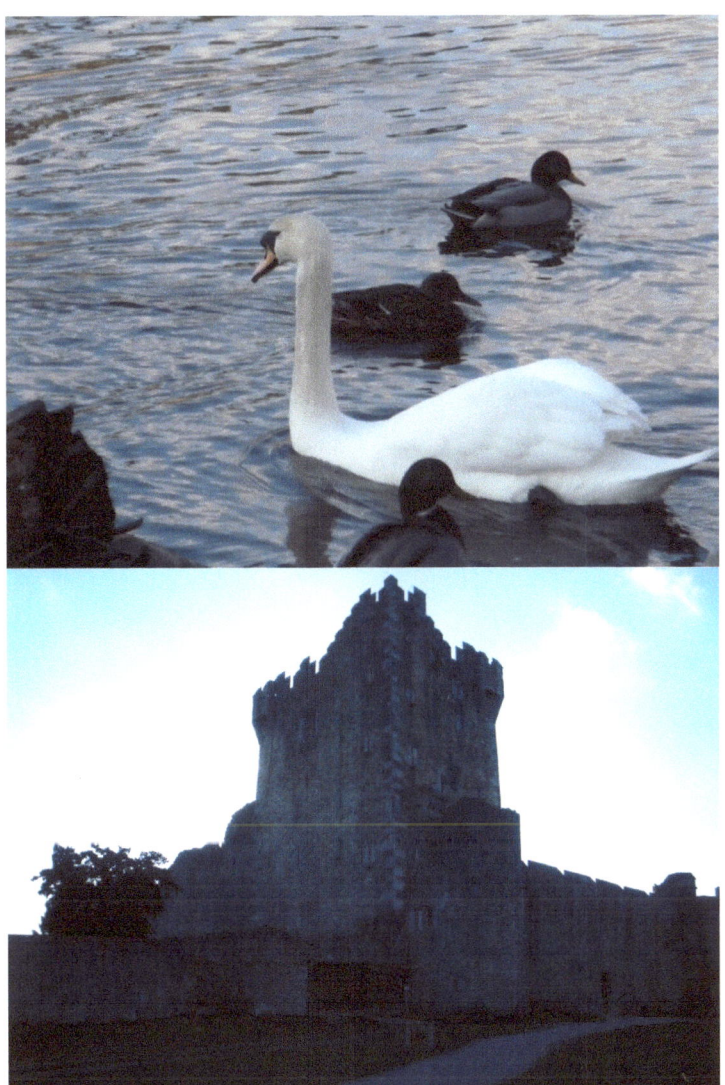

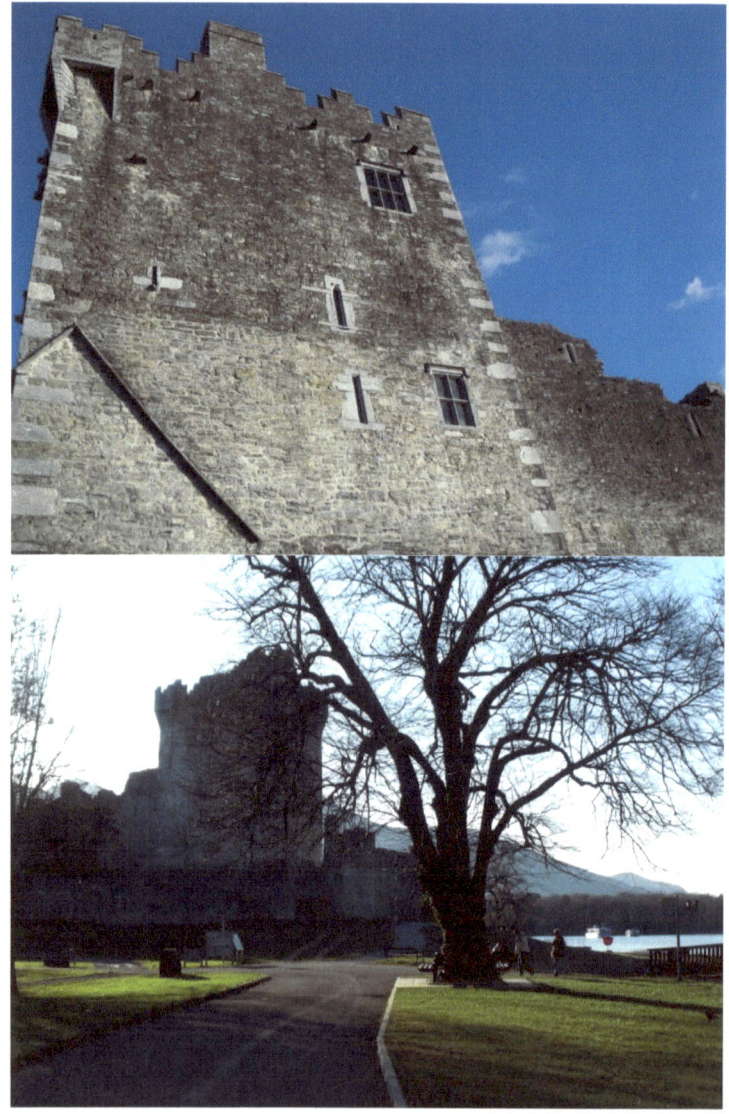

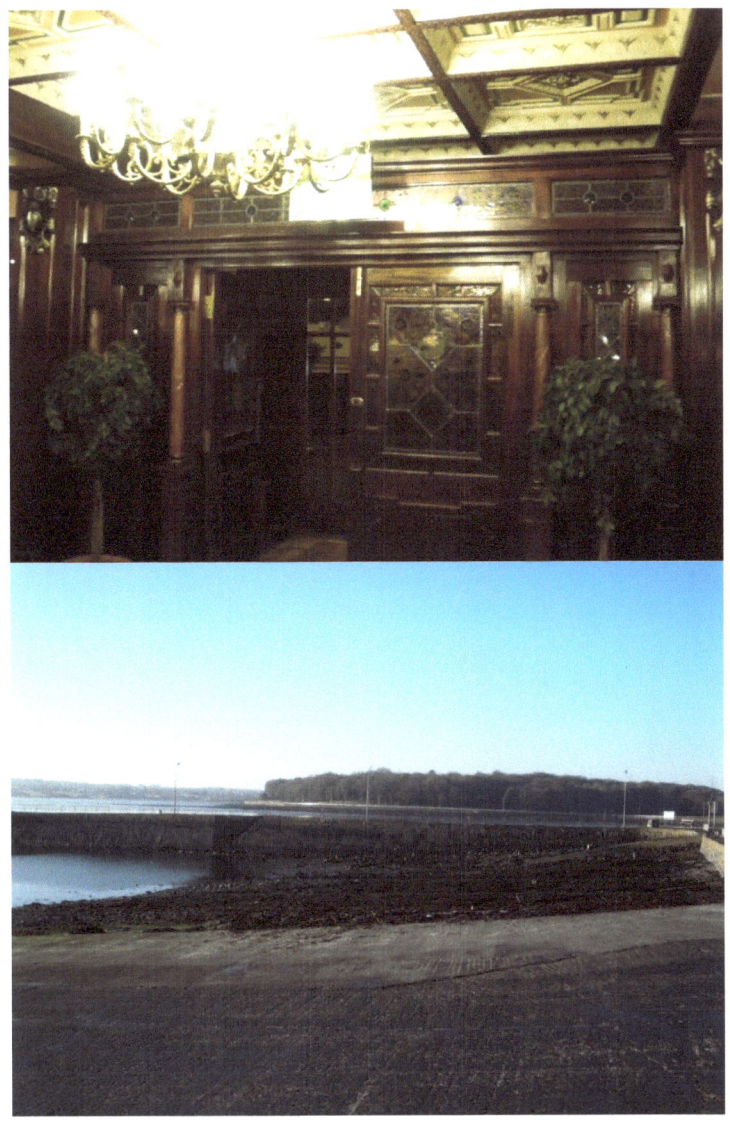

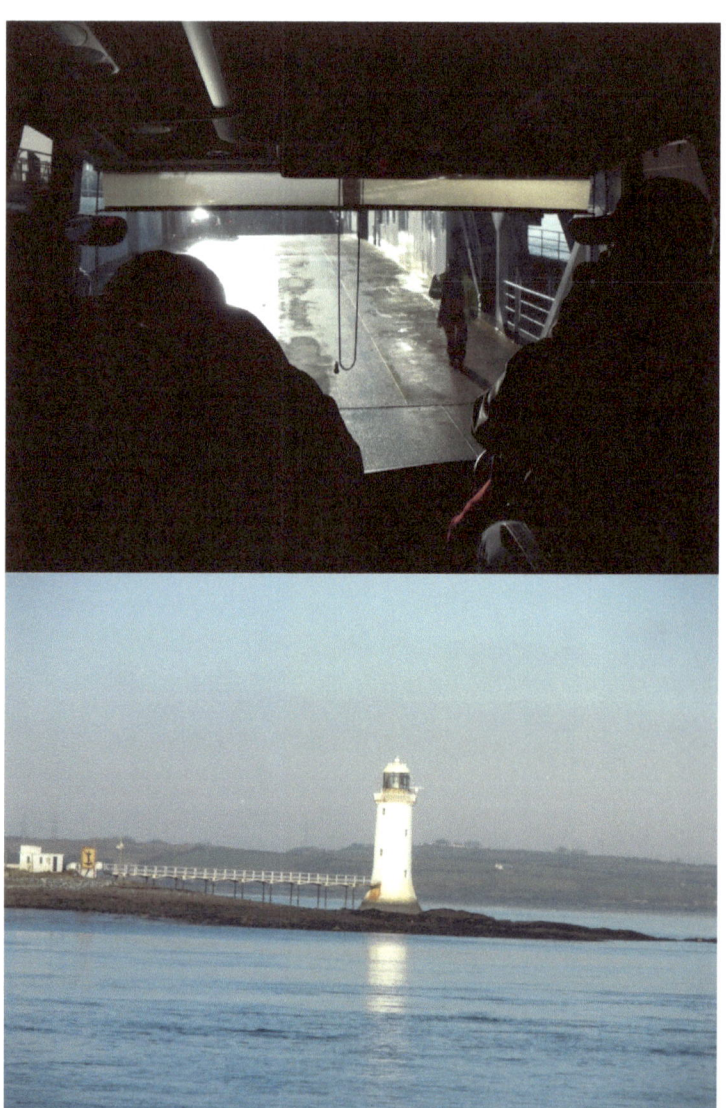

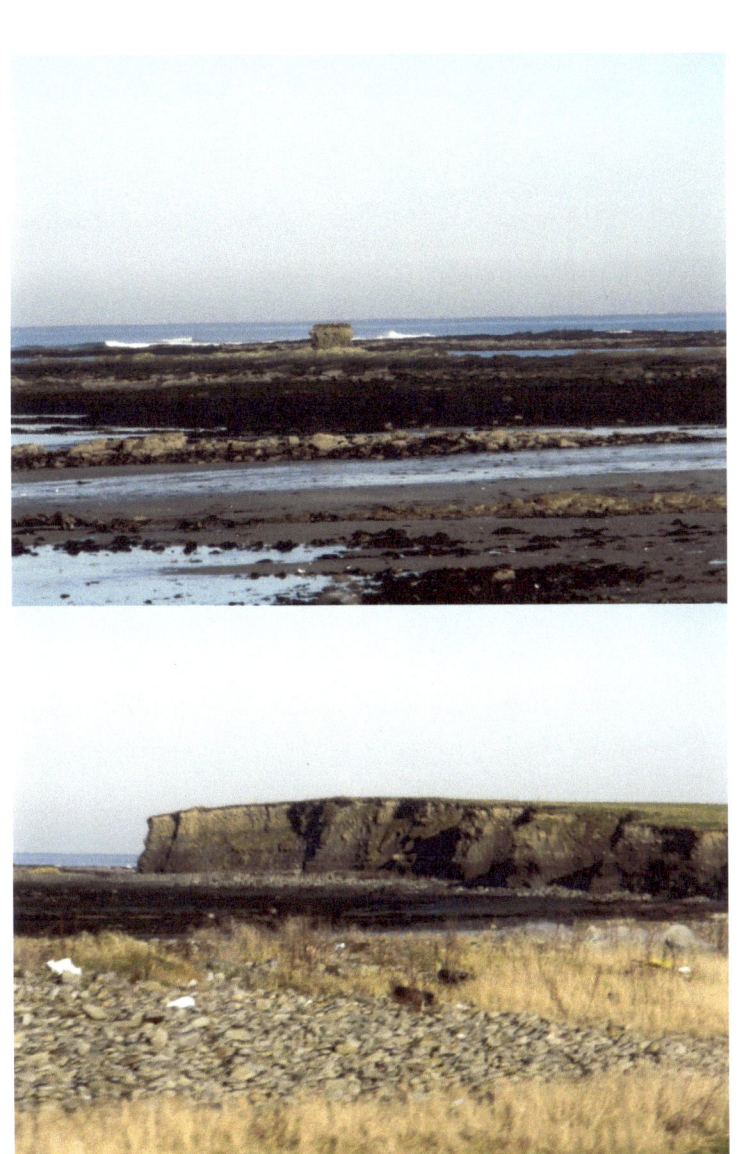

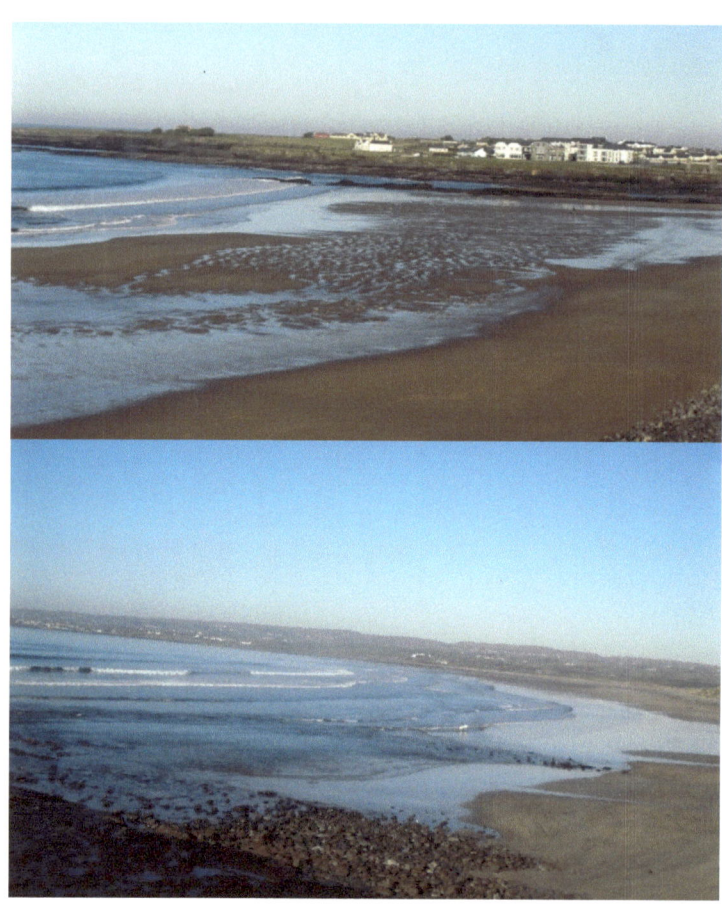

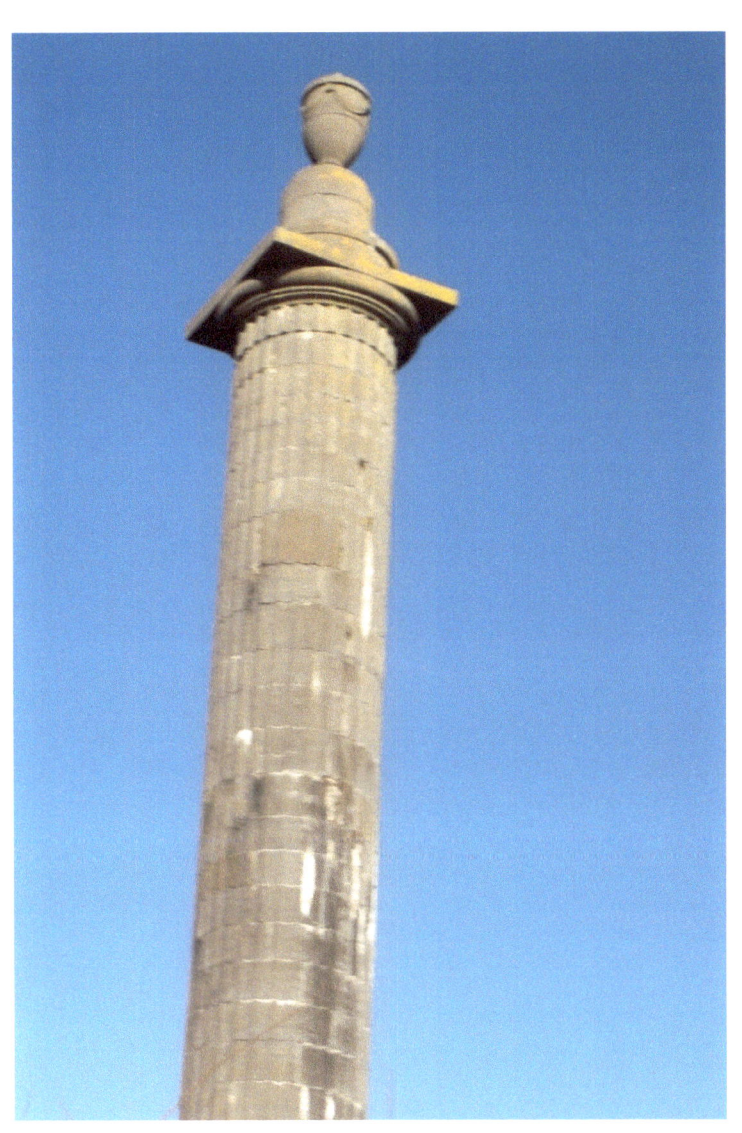

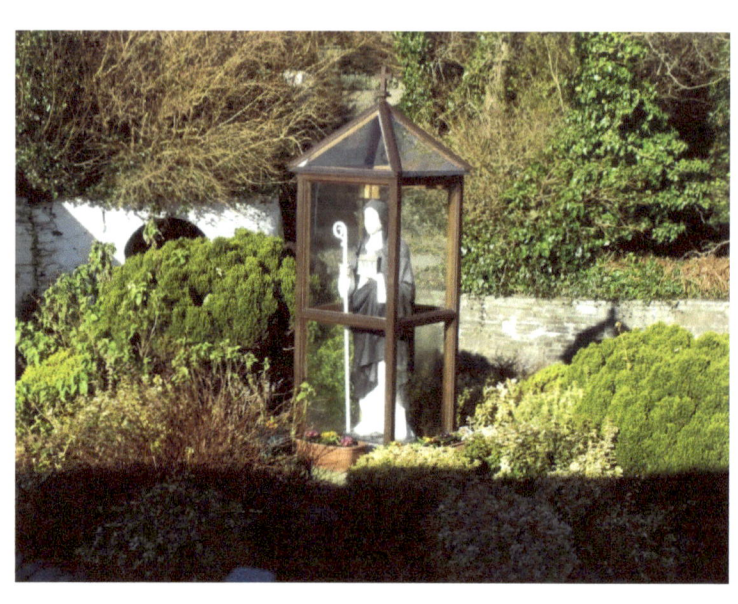

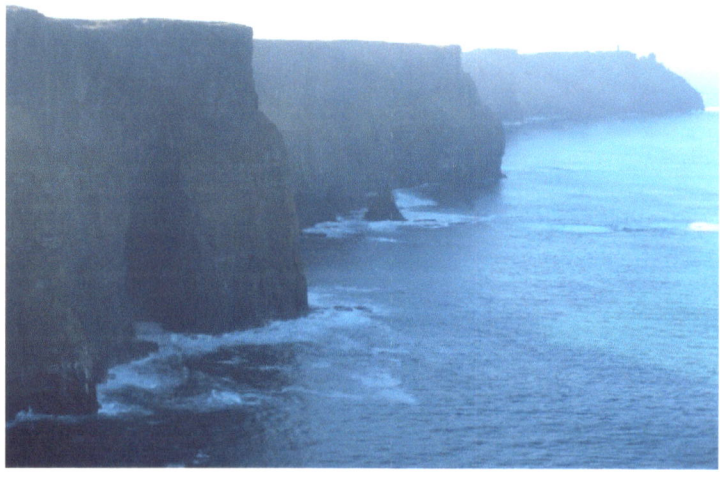

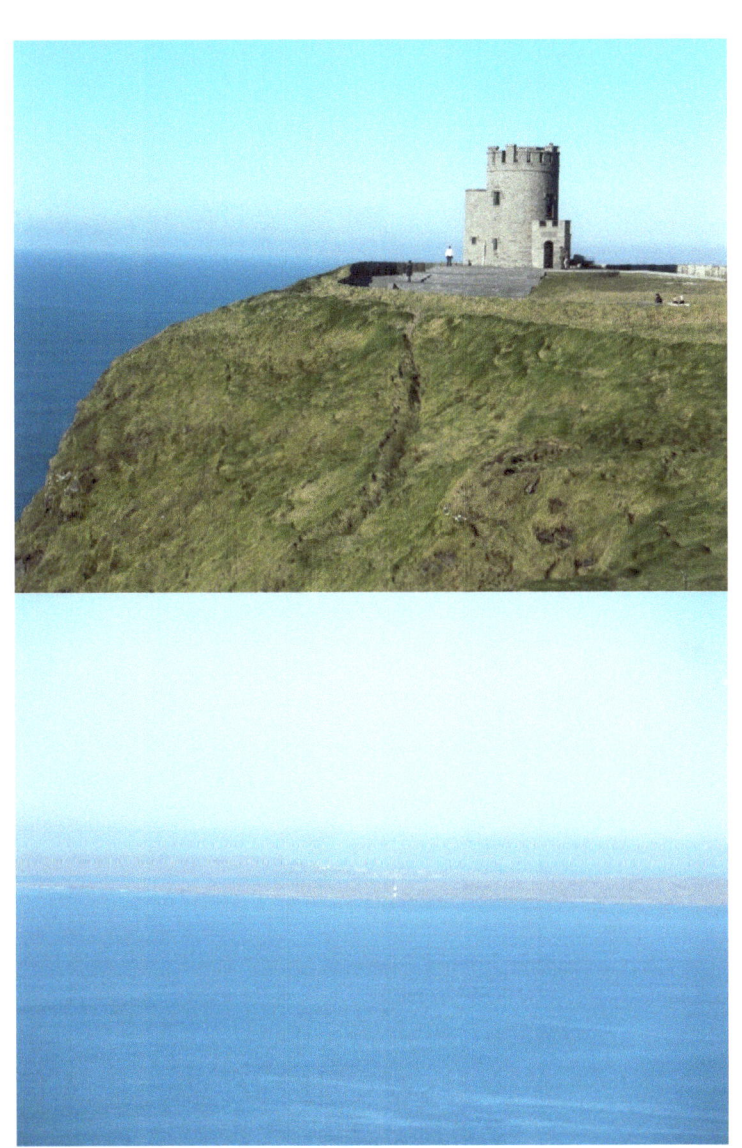

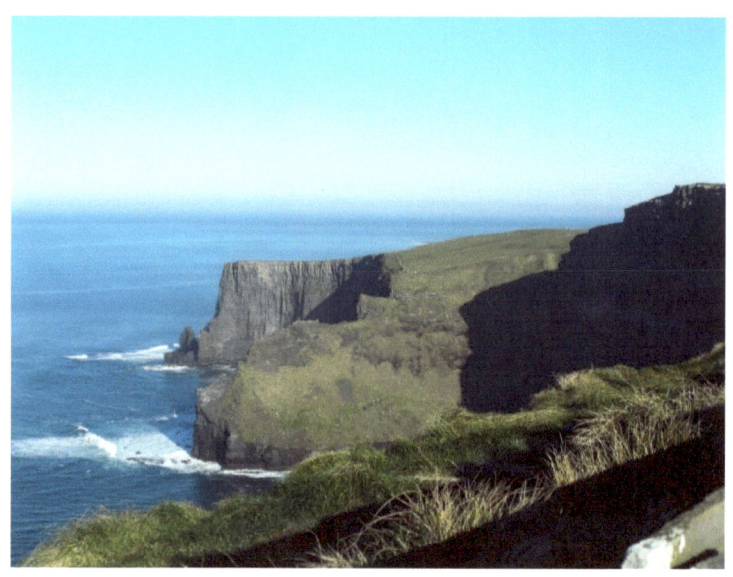

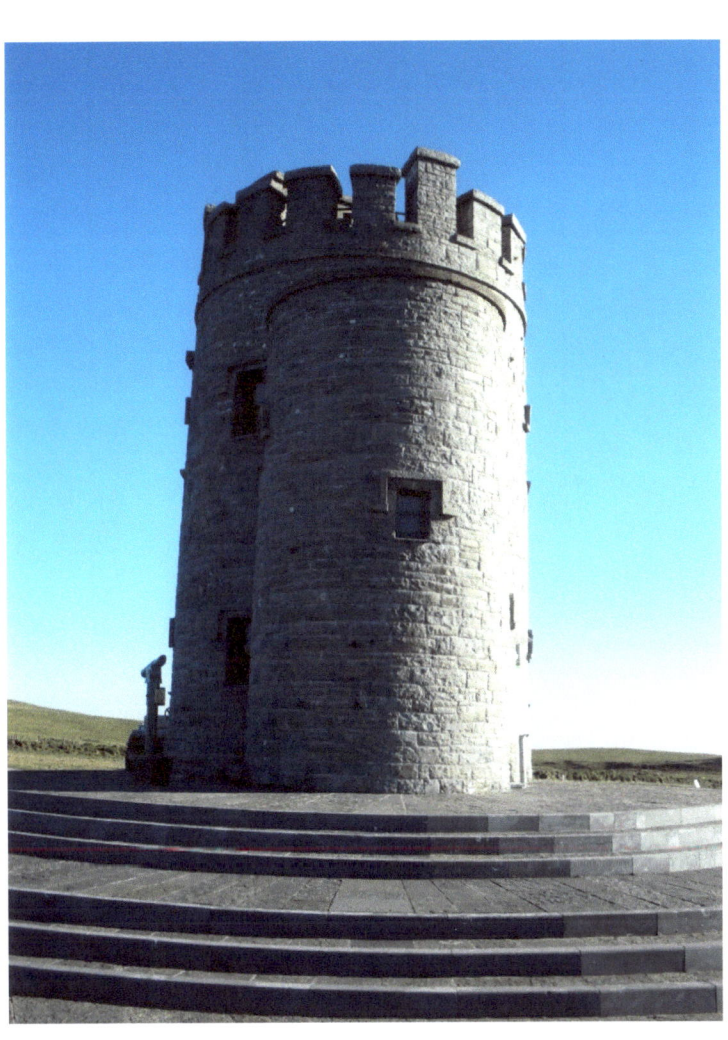

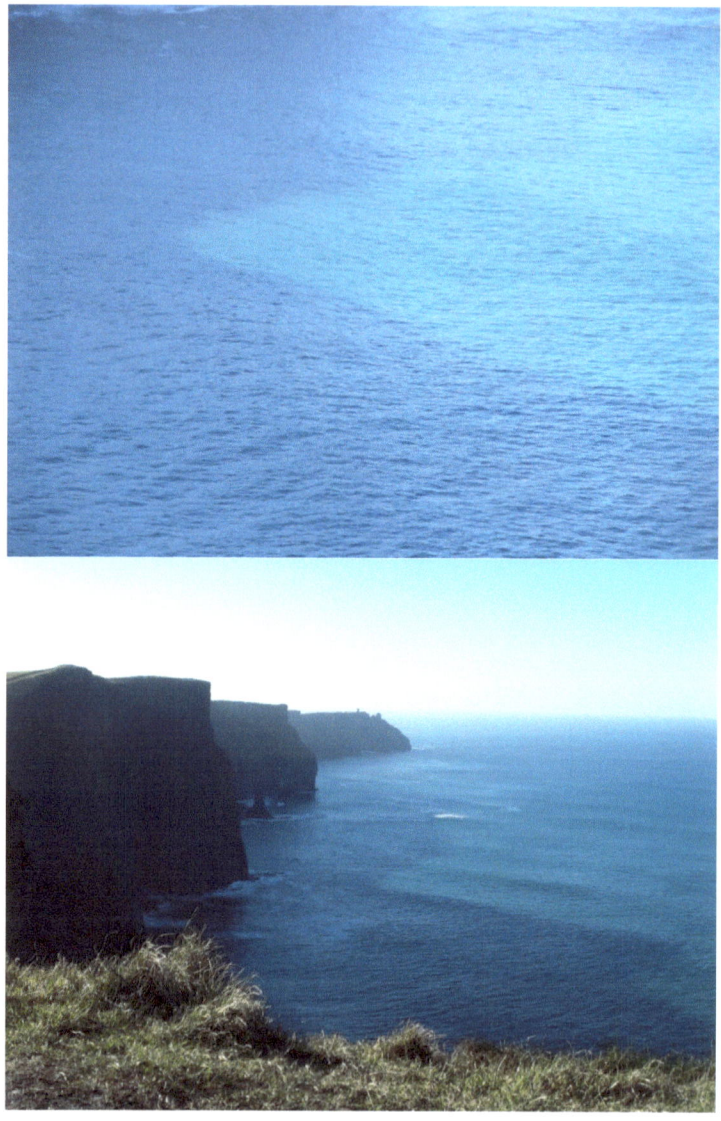

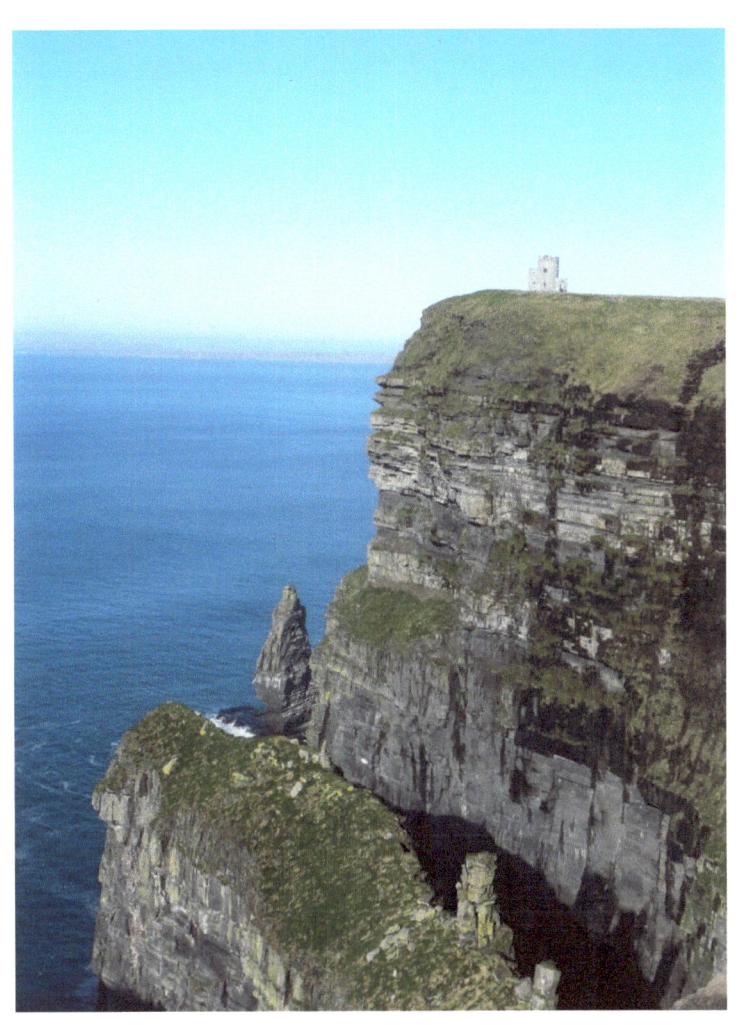

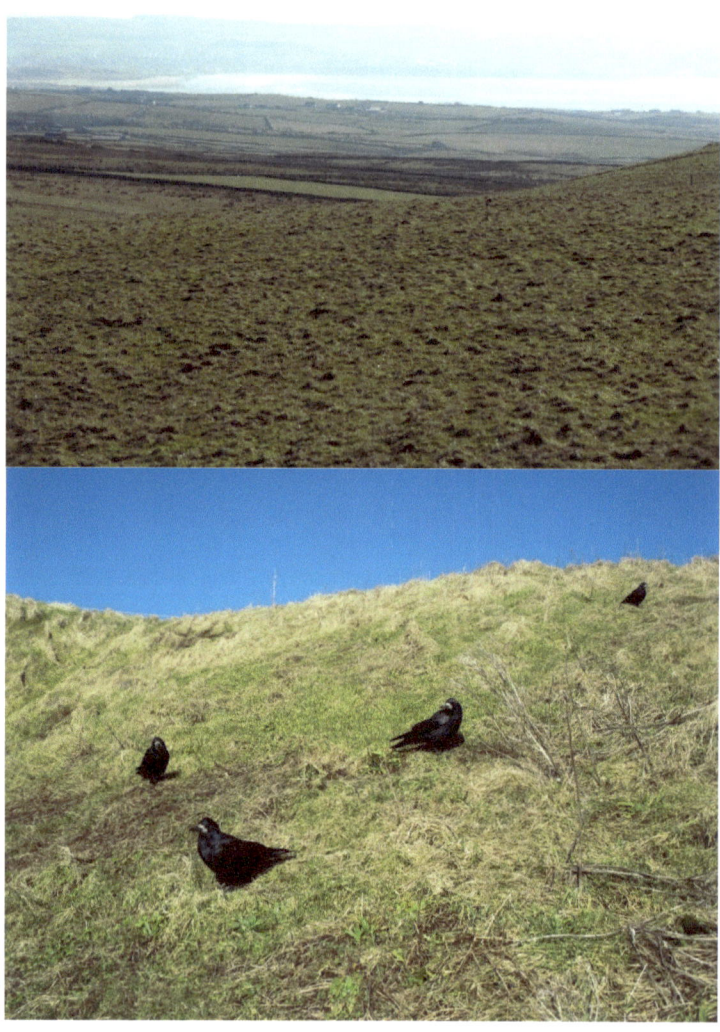

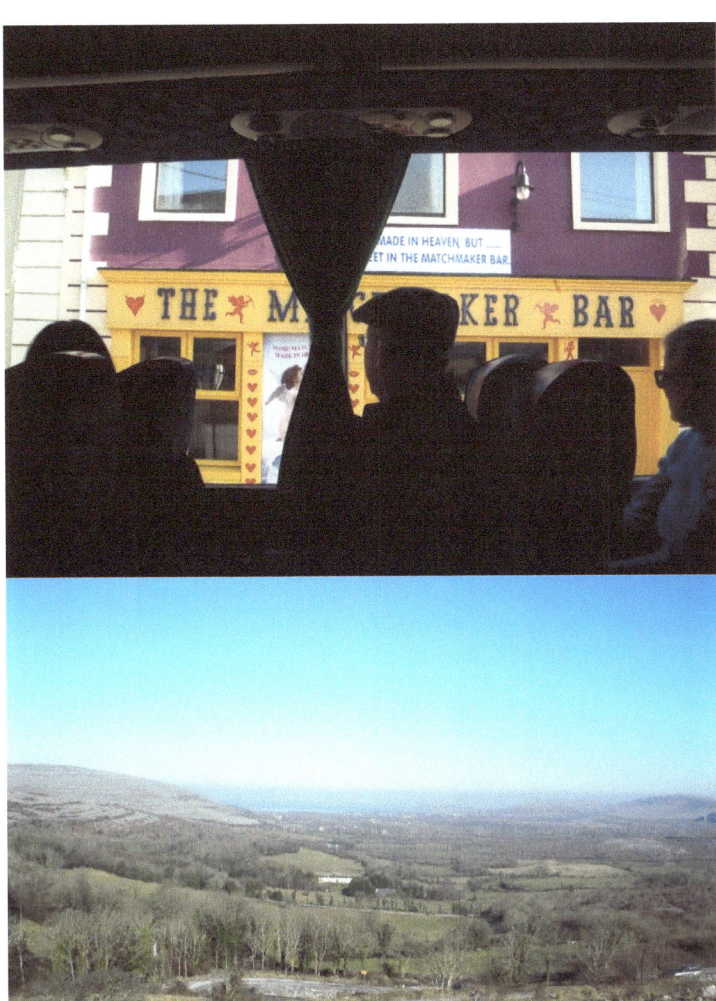

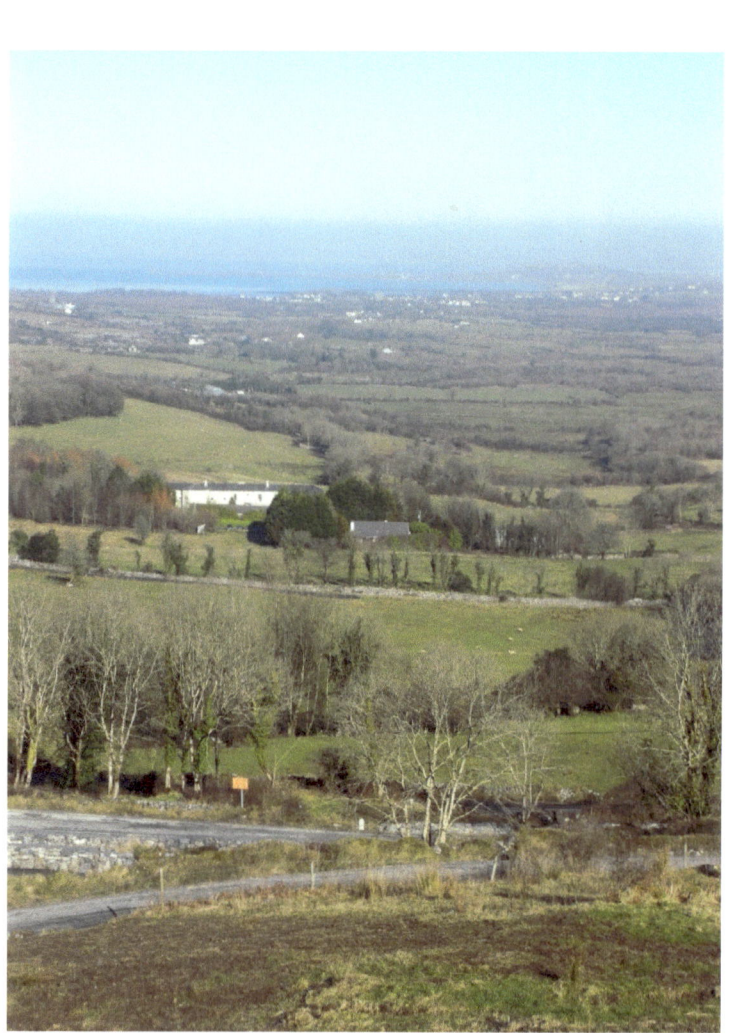

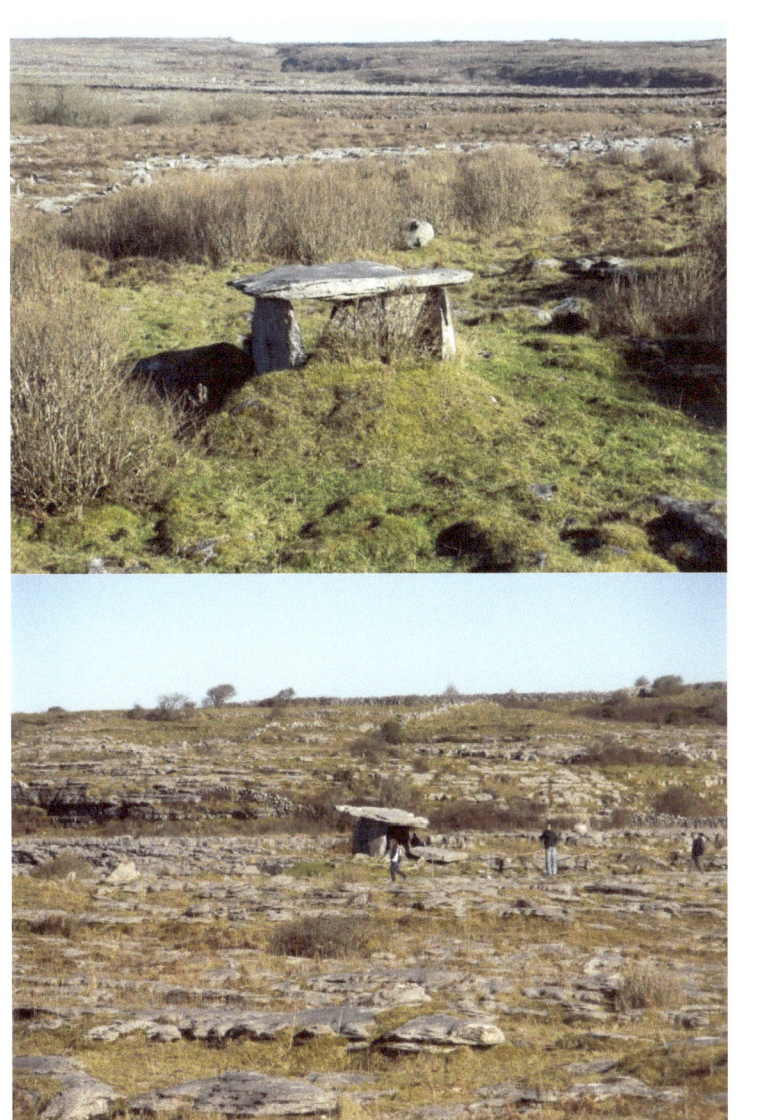

www.ingramcontent.com/pod-product-compliance
Lightning Source LLC
Chambersburg PA
CBHW040829180526
45159CB00001B/118